BIGGER MEN

FOR

BETTER

CHURCHES

by Cleon Lyles

Second Printing

Privately Published by the author

P.O. Box 228
Little Rock, Arkansas

DEDICATION

To the elders of the Downtown church of Christ (Sixth at Izard) in Little Rock, Arkansas, under whose supervision it has been my pleasure to work for nearly seventeen years, this book is affectionally dedicated.

INTRODUCTION

"How will they know it if someone does not say it," was the comment of a friend after he had read a portion of this book, and was asked if it seemed too blunt.

We cannot apologize for the frankness of these chapters, because we believe the thoughts need to be expressed. But with all sincerity we can say no harmful "know it all" attitude was intended.

On a number of occasions the contents of the first five chapters of this book have been given as lectures. Hundreds of brethren, most of them elders, deacons and preachers, have insisted that they should be written. It is our prayer that the good they dreamed of will be done. We express our thanks to them for their encouragement, and to all who have assisted in any way, to make this book possible.

This book is written as a common sense approach, dealing with things that occur in a working agreement between elders and those with whom they labor.

It is our prayer that those who read these pages will receive something that will help in maintaining unity and happiness in their work for the Lord. May the Lord continue to bless us all in our work for Him.

Cleon Lyles
Little Rock, Arkansas. U.S.A.

INDEX

INDEX CONTINUED

CHAPTER I

ELDER-ELDER RELATIONS

The scriptural qualifications for elders are clearly set forth in the New Testament; thus, this chapter is not intended to discuss this aspect of the elder's position nor responsibility. The need for a better understanding from the common sense point of view of the relationship between elders, and their working together in harmonious unison, is the material for discussion. The suggestions presented for consideration are tried and proved to be sound, workable ones, accomplishing the most progress in a satisfactory manner.

Since the harmony, development, and growth of a congregation depend largely upon a proper relationship between its elders, it is of the utmost importance that elders be mutually interested in a spirit of oneness of their purpose in serving together. Churches cannot be disturbed when a strong, closely knit, group of elders is in control of the congregational affairs. When elders are in complete unity, following the New Testament teachings, no harm nor division can interrupt the tenets and progress of the Lord's church.

WISDOM IN NUMBERS

God gives instruction for a plurality of elders for the oversight of a church and even we, with our finite minds, can understand the wisdom in His plan. A prevalent question often presented is how many should be the proper number to best serve in this capacity. There are brethren who believe that every man meeting the scriptural qualifications should be appointed to this office; while there are others who feel that a church should have as few as is possible for getting the congregational work accomplished. Since this question of exact number is not answered in God's Word, the answer is to be found in the needs of an individual church.

There is no value in appointing a large number of men solely for the purpose of having a large governmental board. However, there is lack of common sense in the refusal to appoint enough men needful for properly overseeing the business applicable to the particular congregation. Each church should have the number of elders necessary for accomplishing the work in a proper and efficient and worthy manner. The appointment of a man to an eldership is not done merely for the purpose of doing him personal honor, but for the higher honor of getting the work of the Lord's church done with dignity. Whatever the number of elders required to oversee the business of a given congregation, in the very best interest of that particular church, is precisely the numerical group which should be appointed.

While there are congregations operating efficiently and doing a great work with a minimum number of elders, less than a half dozen, there is one important factor to be considered. It is possible for a church to have a good operative eldership for several years without feeling the need for more appointments, even though it is growing in congregational size, then suddenly find itself with few, or no elders. Within a year, or matter of a few months, several elders may die, or move in location, leaving a church deficient in leadership. Often, in such a given situation, men will be appointed under the pressure of expediency who are not quite prepared for this important work and a church will suffer greatly for several years. It is prudent and wise, therefore, to look to the future in establishing a training program for well chosen younger men in order that they could be ready to assume this leadership when the need arises. Preparedness in exercising such a training program will avert loss of time in the worthy activities of a church program; perhaps, even avert a retrograde movement through lack of strength in a sudden decrease of elder leadership.

PERSONALITY DIFFERENCES

Distinctive personal characteristics will be present in any group of elders since they are human beings. These personality differences, regarding their varying viewpoints and manner of thinking about doing the Lord's work, result from their individual backgrounds in respect to their training, opportunities, secular education, and even business pursuits. The size of a church wherein they grew up will affect their respective characteristic mental attitudes. These differences may either be an asset or liability, help or hindrance, to the work of the congregation where they serve in the capacity of elder.

From a multiplicity of viewpoints can come a more pervasive, all-wise state of planning, developing, and ruling a church when a group of elders exercise a long-suffering attitude toward one another in working together. The man reared in a large, vast operational congregation will present ideas for long range planning; another from a smaller church will naturally act as a monitor in his limited scope, which will be of value in keeping the church they serve on an even keel during its years of growth. However, intense caution should be used to avoid the pitfall of human tendency in thinking for doing things exactly as they were done in a man's home congregation, where he was reared. An elder should be interested and keenly aware of what would be the best course of action, for the church of his youth cannot be the measure for his present age and location; only the sacred scriptures, combined with time and place, should be the measuring rod for the congregation's achievements where an elder serves. The character of growth is controlled by the economy of the present, never the past, with scriptural guidance.

THE RULING ELDER

One elder is equal, in all respects, to his brother-elders in spiritual respective to individual importance. Each elder is subservient to the Lord only, and a servant to the church in his service for overseeing its best interest. There is a grave danger which any group of elders faces in allowing one among them to become the thinker for all the others. A situation like this is unscriptural, unsound, and unacceptable with the Lord. If one elder is going to do all the thinking, decision making, then a one man eldership would be all that is needful. God would have instructed this course of rule in a church had He wanted such an eminent position held by one among the plurality of elders. This condition arises sometimes when proper care has not been shown in the selection of elders and when men who are incapable of co-operating, working with the other leaders as a collective group, have been appointed. Men who would become offended, personally affronted, reacting like children because their individual ideas might not always be acceptable ones, should not be appointed to serve as elders. Each man should understand what is expected of him when he accepts an appointment to the eldership, being ready, willing, and able to set aside his personal feelings when human aspects of personality come into conflict with what is the best interest of the church, super-ceding always his individual position.

The versatility of the ordinary Christian man is the collective intellectuals which the Lord directs should govern, as overseers, in His churches. The authority for a "ruling elder" is not found in God's law. A body of elders is merely a vehicle for making the best decisions possible for an assembly of God's people. Equipped solely with his intelligence, his knowledge of the Bible, and his faithful humility, each elder should present individual ideas for whatever they are worth to his fellow-elders. No one elder is less important, less capable, less worthy than any other.

THE ACTING CHAIRMAN

That all things should be done "decently and in order" is most important in a meeting of a group of elders. The purpose of these meetings is to give a definite plan for procedure and to facilitate the business of a congregation. Thus, a chairman, or presiding elder, for the business meetings should be appointed. This will provide an approved method for conducting meetings in an orderly, expeditious manner; enabling the elders to transact their business meetings with economy of time, with order and accuracy.

The term of office for the chairman should be decided upon by the entire group of elders. Rotation in this position is a necessity in order to avoid an autocratic "ruler" and the danger of getting into a rut. The period of time specified should be adhered to whether it be three months, six months, or a year. However, it is more advisable that the chairmanship be changed at least every six months, and the preference for three month tenures is recommended. Each elder should be willing to serve in this capacity when his time to serve comes about in the rotation system. If an elder does not know the correct procedure for conducting business meetings as chairman, he should be willing to learn.

It is the responsibility of the presiding chairman to begin and close the meetings on time. Too many business meetings operate more in the nature of a fellowship social gathering, with little or no business accomplished; brethren meet, talk in a rather dis-jointed fashion, forgetful of the purpose for their coming together. The acting chairman should follow the parliamentary ruling for order and program, with an observance of a written order of business followed in these meetings. For good ethics and common courtesy, one man should speak at a time after being recognized by the presiding chairman; anyone speaking while another is speaking, reading, or reporting, is not entitled to recognition. It is vitally important that the chairman be in control of the meeting, with respectful compliance from the body of meeting elders, otherwise confusion from incoherant chatter can prevail.

The acting chairman should familiarize himself with the order of business for the current meeting in advance of the elder's assembling. This will enable him to group together all necessary business matters according to their proper order for a more comprehensive presentation. These meetings can best be conducted when the chairman reads all letters received which are pertinent to that particular meeting, and which constitute the portion of their business at hand. The transacted business from the preceeding meeting should be kept in written form, as "minutes," and these minutes should be read before the new business is begun at each session. This procedure should be followed and approved at each regular meeting. The written minutes should be kept as a permanent record and respected in order that no disagreement will be allowed to mar the unity and harmony which must exist between elders. After the minutes are read, from the last meeting, any corrections or additions should be made to these minutes if any are necessary. After the minutes are approved by the elders present, the chairman should sign his name to the record for permanent filing. All decisions that are made should be permanently recorded, even the agreement elders have with a preacher concerning his days off for the purpose of holding meetings, his vacation time, and other matters pertinent to their agreed decisions with the minister. This will eliminate all possibility for future misunderstandings and disputes. It is advisable to have one other elder, in addition to the presiding chairman, sign the completed minutes from each business meeting.

UNANIMOUS AGREEMENT

A roll call should be made in the form of a written record of individual elders present at each business meeting, which is an excellent plan to insure interest and attendance. The majority of the membership present should constitute a quorum for deciding any given question. When there is the ruling that unless all elders agree unanimously on a particular decision, they seldom reach a constructive decision nor accomplish much for the Lord in these meetings. For while the minority is certainly to be considered, the majority in agreement must rule. This conveys the meaning that each elder's opinion should be given courteous attention in their discussing a particular matter together, but the difference in opinion of one or two men should not be able to block any decision which the majority deem would be a wise course of action. After all, if one or two men can control the decisions of the entire eldership by their dissenting voices, one or two men could control both these meetings and the entire state of affairs for the church wherein they serve.

It should be the agreement of each eldership that the majority of those present in their business meetings will carry any given vote, and be the deciding factor in the voting on any decision where there is a difference of opinion. It is to be understood that those who are absent, from a business meeting of the eldership, vote in agreement with the majority; if this agreement is not made, an elder who is absent, by his physical absence, can block the decisions of those present. If an entire eldership is prohibited from accomplishing the work that needs to be done by the vote of one elder's voice, by token of his absence, the life of system and order within the organization is de-defeated. Christian common sense and courtesy should be used with the utmost tact, at all times, in dispatching business in the elder's assembly. Correct procedure is just as necessary in elder's meetings as all God's written rules for orderly conduct in the Lord's business since theirs is the greatest business in the world, overseeing one group of His flock. The acting chairman of these business meetings has the same privilege as any other elder when a decision is to be decided by a vote, since each member of the eldership is individually equal.

SPECIAL APPOINTMENTS

There are two kinds of special appointments: One for deliberation, or investigation, and the other for a specific course of action. When an elder is appointed to supervise the investigation of a certain project, should he consult the other elders before making a firm commitment for some work to done? He certainly should! One man should never be given the power to make any decision alone that will ultimately affect the Lord's work in a church. For example, an elder is appointed to investigate a phase or portion of the work involved in the ramifications for a building program, or some form of remodeling work. This appointment would not give the authority to him for taking action in having any work done, whether it was to tear down, modify, or erect any amount of construction, at his own discretion. This special- appointment would give him no authorization for having any changes made, major or minor, but only to investigate the detail for that portion assigned to him. His only action should be in committing these findings to the entire eldership for consideration and action.

While an appointment for the investigation of some portion of a particular work might necessitate only one elder, the examination and deliberation for an overall project could best be served by at least three men being appointed, and composed of those whose opinions vary. Then, when their examination and deliberation has been thrashed out, exploring all facets of this special project, the plans can be presented to the other elders, at their business meeting, with many trivialities removed which would be a saving of time, for positive decision.

When a special appointment is made for some specific action, which would have to do with a minor decision concerning some operational function of an already established program in a congregation, an elder could be expected to proceed with his work. For example, an elder might be appointed to consider the best method for designating men to wait on the Lord's table and to act upon his own decision. However, this type of authorization would be the only exception to the rule for decisions and other courses of action being confined to a meeting of minds by the joint-elder's assembly.

DIVIDING THE WORK

A wise eldership is one that divides and shares the responsibility for the mental and physical work of the church among themselves. Each elder, according to his individual ability, should participate in, or oversee, a certain phase of the planned work. For illustration, one elder is appointed chairman of the Educational Committee, one to serve in the capacity for overseeing church Publicity, another elder as the chairman of Benevolent Works, and so forth, until the work is equally distributed among the members of the eldership. In this manner, the employment of each elder with a definite responsibility brings intellectual, spiritual, and emotional satisfaction.

After serving as the chairman for one particular phase of their work, for a specified period of time, a rotation system could be established whereby another elder would shift position and accept the responsibility for one of the other given divisions of the program. In this way, each man would have a direct contact with each phase of the work. Of course, this suggestion does not imply that the individuals would operate independently, separate and apart, from the group of elders; but would be responsible for the day-to-day routined work, giving a full report of their activities at the joint-elder meetings. It is inadvisable, even dangerous, when an elder takes the mental attitude that he can make independent decisions and carry out policies apart from his fellow-elders. While the eldership is inhabited by individual Christians, as is the rest of the church, it is imperative that their combined leadership act in a oneness for overseeing the work of a congregation. Each elder needs personal experience in every phase of the Lord's work, but much harm can be done since it is unscriptural, and it should not be allowable, for an elder to act independent of the entire group. In summary, individual service and responsibility assumption for portions of the program is healthy, but collective thinking and activated decisions must be made by the eldership.

CLOSED MINDEDNESS

Elders need to be cautious regarding the closing of their minds against new ideas, concepts, and improved innovations for their programs of work. Since it is the very law of nature that nothing stands still, but is in a constant state of progression or retrogression, so it is true in the development and growth of a congregation. The man who is unwilling to learn, to be mentally alert in accepting new and better ideas, is an elder incapable by his own unwillingness to lead a congregation into greater work. For while it is true that the laws of God stand immutable, it is no less true that customs and manners of the times are constantly being improved, which can enable a church to grow through utilizing these modern domestic conveniences. Commodious developments in material serviceability can be used to serve the Lord's work, when accepted, for promoting more physical comfort for a congregation's membership. For illustration, hard, uncushioned pews do not aid a Christian by physical discomfort in rendering obedient service, during the worship hour, unto his Lord. A dozen, or more, uncomfortable and crying infants in an auditorium, because of the lack of a nursery room, add no glory to the service.

Several years past our buildings, with their limited educational plants, did not cost more than fifty, or seventy-five, thousand dollars; with most of them being built for even far less than this amount. However, even the construction of the same buildings today, with the bare commodious essentials, would cost two or four times more than the amount of expenditure involved twenty years ago. For elders to close their minds against the present day public increase in building costs, refusing to allocate, or spend, the necessary amount for an adequate edifice in which their congregation can grow, would be to utterly fail in their duty for the present generation. There is considerable basis for the conclusion that more money should be spent for better educational facilities and the controlling question is often evidenced among elders as to whether the church economy is best served by providing a substantial budget increase for building expansion and improvement. Leadership requires courage, boldness, and the willingness to act on faith in an expansion program.

The discussion of salaries is expounded in another chapter, but what is meant by the expression "closed minedness" is best illustrated here by a casual mentioning of present day increase in living costs over the past generation in the national economic situation. Sometimes an elder has worked for many years without earning a large sum of money, yet during his working years the sum which he earned in wages represented a good, liveable salary. This elder retires, his family has been reared and is individually financially independent; his wants and needs are fewer, and with his expenses considerably lessened, he is able to live comfortably on a pension, or income from former years' savings. Naturally, it would be easy for this elder to be blinded to the demands from current expenses that are involved in the present day rearing of a family. It is human for this man to be unaware of the need for increased salaries of the paid employees in the church; no one would have dreamed that the dollar value of the present day would be less than half its value of twenty years past. However, since the national economy has changed, with a continued increase in all living expenses, elders cannot close their minds concerning the facts of the material life of society, refusing to support the physical needs of their employees, without doing harm to the congregation's spiritual life, also.

An eldership that is closed minded regarding the church budget, ignoring a planned method for contributions from the membership, is erroneously rejecting our example in Divine history, written and left for Christian instruction. When elders refuse to adopt what is generally called the "budget system" and reject the acceptance of pledging, they retreat from the scriptural example found in the purposing of the Corinthian church. The closed minded men who would say that the denominations do it that way, practice a form of pledging and budgeting, are using unwise reasoning as the opium of human thinking. Denominations use doors, lights, windows in their buildings and elders do not reject the usage of these commodities when planning the architectural design for their buildings. Denominations practice public prayer in their respective services of worship, but our brethren do not refuse to abstain from rendering this form of service to God because the denominational groups do so. Thus, such an argument against using individual pledging in establishing a scripturally approved method for the basis of a church budget is not sound thinking, but reveals an unwillingness to accept Bible examples for a guidance counselor. This determined human unwillingness is, of course, fatal to the concept of leadership and under which a church will ultimately suffer in future growth.

Among all the tragic consequences of age and other human failures, the suppression of progressive thinking for the betterment, development, and growth of a church is among the most poignant.
When an elder adamantly refuses to move from the antiquated past,
where he has pegged or bogged down, in his mental capacity
for progressive thinking, it is recommended that the eldership move
forward without this one man being allowed to deter their plans
for growth. A retreat from stimulated leadership arises in part
from a profound misinterpretation of Christian development and the
growth of a congregation can be retarded if an elder who is suffering from the spiritual disease is allowed to hinder its progress. Of
course, an elder who has the true heart of a Christian, with the cause
of Christ as core and center of his life, will be willing for a church
to progressively move forward while he prayerfully meditates for
a better understanding of the situation. When an older man, in childish determination, stands in opposition, to the growth of a congregation, the eldership must remember that the Lord's work is bigger
than one man. Human age nor a closed, determined, "human-
minded" elder should not be allowed to create strife in an eldership that is dedicated to do its best work in serving the Lord's church.

PERSONAL JEALOUSY AND ENVY

The Lord condemns jealousy, and envy, both which create disunity and strife. It would seem that such human errors should not
plague the members of an eldership; yet, as long as men live in the
flesh, these weaknesses of the flesh shall continue to strive among
them. In these instances when the evils of jealousy distinguish themselves among the elders, a serenity of spirit cannot be achieved until the offenders become the masters of their own attitudes and personal actions. The insidious actions which stem from envy among
elders manifest this emotional disorder in several ways. An example
of such attitudes is well illustrated by the experience related by a

preacher who had once suffered with two elders because of their immature jealousy over his visits with them. Whenever this preacher
would pay an individual call upon one of these two elders, he felt
the unhealthy compulsion to visit with the other man immediately in
order to placate him, or to keep the one whom he had failed to visit
from becoming hurt and peevish. Unless he called upon both these
elders on the same day, the "fat was in the fire!" and it would take
days to pacify the offended elder. Of course, such an extreme condition of childish behaviour is unusual, but such was the case. By apply-
ing intelligence and good judgment, elders can succeed in living
wisely, without fear of un-Christian jealousies tormenting the relationship among them.

Envy of a preacher's popularity with the congregation is not an
uncommon element of personal disturbance with some elders. In a
certain city, a preacher was doing an outstanding work, both in the
community and in the church, everybody liked and appreciated him
for his goodness. The business men of the community thought well
of him, the congregation loved him, and the church was growing in
spiritual development as well as in membership. Jealousy in the
hearts of some of the elders over-ruled Christian love, and sound
judgment, causing the dismissal of this preacher, which injustice
gave him grief that it took years for him and his family to overcome.
In addition to doing this church great harm, the value of Christianity suffered in the eyes of the community. What havoc can be wrought
for a church and its people by jealousy within an eldership when some little men try to fill a big place and are not big
enough to do it! This malignant condition is best expressed by a
poet when he said, "With that malignant envy, which turns pale
and sickens, even if a friend prevail; which merit and success pursues with hate, and damns the worth it cannot imitate."

THE "SENIOR" ELDER

The Bible says nothing about a "senior elder," this terminology is foreign to the sacred scriptures, but churches have been ruled by him, and hurt because of him. When this term of eminence is applied to an elder, it is used to convey respectful honor for his age and years of service in a church. However, there are some few instances when a dominant, forceful personality which generates activity by a man and not merely his age in years creates the application of "senior" elder for himself by others. The repetition of this appellation, over a period of time, can dangerously come to mean more than is applied to both the individual elder and the church members. Addressing a man as the "senior elder" sets him apart from the other elders, inadverently giving him a pre-eminent position which is contrary to God's designed plan that one elder should not be above other elders. While a man of age in years and experience should know more, exemplifying a greater depth of wisdom than a younger man who has served for less time as an elder, there are some cases of the rule of years not holding true. The passing of years should bring more wisdom, but sometimes years pass bringing only age and nothing more.

Wise is the man who grows in grace and knowledge, with the passing years of age, who understands that his length of service as an elder brings the obligation of sharing his knowledge with others. Humble, worthy, and filled with wisdom is the man who does not expect the seniority of his age, or experience, to set him above his fellow elders. Often this unintended pre-eminence is bestowed upon an elder without his intention, or awareness, of its taking place; the preacher, or some other elder, may be responsible for it. Wise is the elder who refuses to allow this to happen, or who rejects the misconstrued honor, when he becomes aware of such an existing situation. Great wisdom is exercised, also, by other elders who are keenly aware of the possibility of this misconception among themselves and are cautious to prevent, or stop it, whichever the case may be. God did not appoint "senior" and "junior" elders in His church; He appointed elders.

SELECTING NEW ELDERS

The selection of elders is a major decision which will always present peculiar problems in certain aspects. The Lord gave instruction for appointing elders, but He gave no specific plan for the manner in which they are to be selected. Thus, in the absence of Divine instruction, we must use common sense in our approach to this subject.

There are some Christians, in some congregations, who attempt to use the selection of the seven men to serve tables, in the early apostolic church, as a basis for their example; it is most doubtful that this is an example for our pattern to follow in selecting elders. There are some who believe that the ruling elders should select other elders; there are others who believe in the practice of selecting elders from the names submitted by the congregants, which they have written on cards distributed for this purpose. The selection of men to serve as elders is a responsibility which should be shared by both the present elders and the congregational members. The method of selection by name suggestions, written and handed in on cards, presents several undesirable aspects. The primary danger in this method is the fallicy of people suggesting the names of their close friends whom they love, but which love of friendship may blind them to some personal weaknesses that would render their esteemed friend incapable of serving as a worthy elder. The outcome can result in needed explanations and hurt feelings for the persons involved. However, if a period of proper study by the congregation as a whole precedes the selection of elders, this method can be fruitful.

There are devout Christian men who would meet the scriptural qualifications for appointment to an eldership, but who would not, for one of several reasons, be able to work in the program of a given congregation. When a group of elders is directing a church in a program that is scripturally healthy, growing, and prospering, it would be folly to select a new man who would present abrupt changes in its method of doing the work. Individuals vary enormously in background, in their personal manner of thinking as to how the business of the Lord's work should be accomplished, and when such individual personality differences would not fraternize or blend harmoniously with an eldership, this man could not serve well their program.

The method recommended, which has proven to be successful, for selecting new men to serve in the capacity of elders is for the group of serving elders to select men who are qualified scripturally for consideration. Following the choosing of these names, the elders talk with them privately and individually in order to ascertain whether or not they are willing to be appointed to this work, and to become acquainted with their respective viewpoints concerning the program that is under operation in that particular church. After this has been accomplished, with quietness and dignity, the men who have consented to have their names submitted to the congregation by their willingness to work in the program should be presented to the membership. The congregation should then be given a specified period of time for consideration of the men suggested, during which time any criticism may be presented to the elders. All criticism must be identified by the complaintant member, either in written form or personal discussion, with one of the serving elders. There are instances when some sincere member of the church has opposed the appointment of a qualified man on the basis of some personal misunderstanding, which can be clarified after a discussion with one of the elders and without the man whom they have criticized needing to suffer the knowledge of such misunderstanding. After the elders and congregational members are satisfied that the men whose names have been considered are well qualified to lead and direct the affairs of their church, the approved appointments are made final.

GROWING TOO OLD TO SERVE

The difficult question which often must be faced is when is a man too old to serve competently as an elder, and how to handle this ticklish situation when, and if, it arises. Nature often so deceptively changes a man's ability to think, with accurate co-ordination, that the change is hidden from the one who is affected. It is possible for a man to grow too aged to serve acceptably, both mentally and physically, in his capacity as an elder. While some men are young in heart, clear-minded, and bright-eyed at age eighty years, others may become senile and feeble by the time they reach seventy years of age. The answer to "when is an elder too old?" is to be decided in each individual case. When a man ceases to be conscious of competence, refusing in childish pouting to have visions of the needs for continual growth of the church, or when he becomes mentally, or physically, incompetent to work with the other elders in their program, he has grown too old for active service in leading a congregation. It is fortunate when an elder is cognizant of his own inability and requests to be released from his responsibility for serving in an eldership. However, if an elder does not recognize his failings by token of agedness, continuing to fill his alloted space in the eldership of a church, the other elders need to lead him quietly while they continue leading the program of the congregation.

ELDERS AND THEIR WIVES

The wife of an elder may be the greatest human inspiration in his life, and his other-half in matters relative to their materialistic business, but the business of the church privacy is a solemn oath with him which must exclude her. She understands that in affording privacy to her husband in his relationship to the eldership, involving the intimate matters which this work often entails, she is merely assuring him the faith which he deserves. The wife of an elder is not scripturally qualified to make decisions regarding the work of a congregation over which her husband serves. There have been instances when an elder was unable to make a decision until he had first consulted with his wife; other instances of an elder being in agreement with a particular decision of the eldership, but who reversed his decision at their next meeting because he had discussed the subject with his wife during the interim of time between meetings. This kind of defensive, dependent elder will never produce reliable leadership.

The degree of information which an elder should devulge to his wife concerning the business is discussed in an elder's business meeting is exactly what is proper and best for public knowledge, no more and no less. There are three primary reasons for matters of an elder's church business not being discussed with his wife, nor related in his conversation at home. First it is lack of consideration for his wife in view of the mental and emotional burden which knowledge of delicate matters will place upon her. She will be duty bound to her husband, as well as to the best interest of the church, not to mention this information, even in a discussion with her closest friend; which restraint may cause embarrassing moments for her when she is fearful of an ordinary conversation for conscientious concern of speaking unwisely. The feeling for unnecessary security and guarded conversations can thus be avoided by the surrender of her husband from his selfishness in laying this burden at her feet. Second, the most tragic consequence of an elder relating all the intimate details of a business meeting to his wife, some matters that are private and not best for common knowledge, is that should she betray his confidence she may create an unintentional disturbance within the harmony of the church.

The third and perhaps most important reason for elders excluding their wives from all knowledge of the internal business discussed within the eldership, unless such information is for public disclosure, is that the Lord did not instruct overseeing of a church to be done by elders and wives. While wives of men qualified to serve as elders play a most important role in respect to their husband's scriptural qualifications, the holy injunction regarding their positions in the elder's service life is that they be "grave, not slanderers, sober, faithful in all things." The most sound suggestion that can be offered is that the privilege of privacy should be extended to an elder by his wife, and an elder to his wife as well as to other members of the congregation wherein he serves and wherein they both worship.

ADVICE FROM AN ELDER

The intelligent suggestions from an elder, respected by all for his faithful service and depth of wisdom, regarding elder-elder relationship is this: "Elders should not allow themselves to be romanced nor courted by individual members within the congregation. An eldership should not be swayed by pressure groups from without nor within the church. Individual elders should avoid personality clashes, and when there does arise a difference of human opinions, a scriptural elder will rise above the human variance, esteeming the good of the Lord's church as all important. The elders in the group should hold each other in the highest personal regard as servants of the Lord, with the common bond of love for His church above all other interests. An elder should not be guilty of making even the most casual remark of having been for something, but over-ruled in the decision made because the other elders were against it. Defend the decisions you make at the right time and in the right place — the meeting of your eldership — forever after holding your tongue and peace. Whenever an elder sells his individualism short, by his sniveling, quippy remarks, he lays the ax at the roots of Christian leadership. Finally, in summary, stay close to God and you will stay close to each other."

WORTHY OF HONOR

God's appointed shepherds, elders serving faithfully in overseeing affairs in the Lord's churches, are worthy of much honor. The Word of God bestows honor upon these men, and commands this respect for them from His people. No man nor group of men does a more important, inspiring, selfless, and worthy work. The hours of prayerful, laborious effort involved in the individual service which an elder offers up to God, through the church he serves, are invaluable and beyond the power for human estimation.

The suggestions and recommendations contained within the pages of this chapter are not intended as an exploitation of one of the Lord's honorable servants. All expressed recommendations are tendered in the spirit of deep humility, and respect, with the prayerful hope that these diversified discussions, regarding varied problems of an elder's working status and human relationship, will be better clarified through distributive information.

"This is a true saying, If a man desire the office of a bishop, he desireth a good work." The highest honor promised by our Father to persevering and faithful elders is, "And when the chief Shepherd shall appear, ye shall receive a crown of glory that fadeth not away."

CHAPTER II

ELDER-PREACHER RELATIONS

Equally important in the scriptural injunctions concerning the harmony which should exist in elder to elder relations are exhortations regarding the importance for unity between elders and preachers. In addition to the immense enrichment of their human relationship, the proper respectful consideration among this group of men will be a limitless power in their combined influence over the spiritual development of a congregation. A harmonious co-existance will be a tremendous asset in developing refined characteristic traits within both the minister and the individual elders, as they share the absorption of their combined work, resulting in the highest degree of human companionship known to mankind while promoting the greatest possible attainments for God. Where affection and reciprocal respect is lacking between a preacher and the elders, they not only contradict the Lord's Will, but their disunity will be a degenerate factor working against their hope for doing the good work to which they aspire within the church they serve.

The following problems, of various natures, that are the most prevalent reasons which hinder a close understanding between elders and preachers are defined and discussed, with suggestions for solutions of these temperaments and attitudes.

THE PREACHER . . . A SERVANT, NOT SUBORDINATE

A preacher is no less a human being who needs compassionate understanding and frequent encouragement, even though a dedicated man to the peculiar work of serving God's created people, than other Christians. His discouragement and even infrequent moments of despair, by the pressures of human emotions, occasionally needs the same amount of expressed appreciation which is the useful lubricant for oiling the machinery of human relations as any other individual member of the congregation. He is a servant of the Lord and though his work is under the supervision of the elders in a local church, he is not subservient to them. The preacher is under no more obligation to his elders than they are obligated to him as colleagues in the business of saving souls and promoting the growth of the congregation they serve together. The major difference in their working conditions is that a preacher is devoting all his time, full time, to preaching the gospel of Christ, and answering daily the calls for help which in substance reflect the whole spectrum of human difficulty. For his full time labor, he receives financial support from the congregation under whose elders he serves, whereas the elders earn their salaries from secular occupations.

EMPLOYMENT OF A PREACHER

The responsibility for engaging a preacher is one of the most important, difficult, tasks for an eldership, involving several reasons for this decision being an arduous assignment. First, there are more congregations needing competent preachers than there are men qualified to fill this demand. Second, while the church is a universal phenomenon in all churches having the uniqueness of sameness in basic principles, each congregation is individual with respect to having both scriptural independence and human peculiarities. One preacher's successful experience can be another's misalliance in a particular location, because the human requirements of a church can be served better by one minister's personality than by those of another man. Thus, it is important for elders to cautiously select the preacher whose personality characteristics will best serve the membership requirements of their congregation. Third, a frequent prerequisite of congregants for hiring a preacher who has established a notable reputation for himself, through several years of experience in the ministry, can infect the elders with this same desirous demand for notoriety. However, elders should remember that each preacher must have a beginning point, a starting place, for building his notable reputation the same as a man in any other field of work; they should not fail to consider a minister who could be exactly the one needful for their con-gregation.

The manipulation of seeking for and engaging a preacher is no small undertaking, without a formula that can be used as an easy so-lution for accomplishing this mission. When elders begin their search for a minister to serve their congregation, they naturally originate their inquiry with preachers known to be successfully active. Often the inquisitorial elders create a feeling of mistrust, or resentment, from the eldership where either a preacher is sought, or information for rec-ommendation of a preacher is requested. In compliance with scrip-tural commandment for Christian unity in the brotherhood and in or-der to avoid this pitfall of resentfulness among brethren, it is sug-gested that the elders and preacher who enjoy the satisfaction of work-ing together be guardians of their cherished compatibility so that such an opportunity for new horizons will not disturb their house-hold. The sanctity of their happiness need not be threatened by such an inquiring from an outside source when there is a harmonious state of existence within an elder and preacher relation. However, it is recommended that the elders engaged in the ticklish errand of seeking a preacher use discreetness and Christian courtesy during their search for a minister who would best meet their requirements.

The method which is generally used in parading several preachers before a church in practicing "try out" sermons Sunday after Sunday, week in and week out, is not recommended as being the best one for either the congregation or the preachers who make this attempt at ac-quaintanceship. The suggested arrangement, as a better procedure for securing a preacher, is for the elders to go hear a man in whom they are interested preach in his own location; investigate him personally and his work in the community where he has been serving. This avoids confusion within their own congregation by advancing preacher after preacher, for weeks on end, before the membership. It is fairer in judging the personality of an individual's preaching ability, also. While some men may be able to give a better performance in a "try out" sermon, the general rule is that most preachers cannot   preach their best lessons under the pressure of this type operation.   When, after hearing a preacher in his own familiar surroundings, the elder's investigation has been satisfied in their belief that a particular   man has been located who can best serve the needs of their congregation, then is the time to invite this preacher to visit in their church and de· liver a sermon.

WORKING AGREEMENTS BETWEEN
ELDERS AND PREACHER

All details relative to their current program and future plans for development should be discussed by the elders with a preacher prior to beginning their work together. The   elders and preacher should have an understanding from the onset of the minister's engagement re- garding the allotted time for him to be away from his local work in evangelistic meetings, lectureships, mid-week meetings which would not involve Sunday services, and his annual vacation. It is advisable that these agreements be put into writing to be kept as a permanent record for the duration of time that an employed preacher works with a particular congregation. This serves both the preacher and the elder- ship in avoiding any future misunderstandings concerning all the a- greements established between them; through a lapse of memory dis- agreements can arise when only verbal assignments are contracted. If, or when, there needs to be alterations or changes made in their origi- nal agreement, these changes should be stabilized in writing, also, after such amiable decisions have been made. The sanctity of all agreements should be honorably kept in the actions of both the preach- er and the elders, with absolutely no breach of contract nor personal violation on the part of either parties.

PARTICIPANTS IN BUSINESS MEETINGS

There is but one exception to the wisdom, as well as common sense thinking, for the minister of a congregation being excluded as a permanent member of all the business meetings of an eldership. This exception being when such a meeting is for the express purpose of discussing the preacher personally. Since the aim of elders' business meetings is for employing whatever stratagem is necessary for planning the program, work, and growth of their congregation, it is imperative that the preacher whose life's work is involved in these plans for operation be included. A preacher must be fully informed regarding all phases of the operational affairs and future plans of the church he serves if he is to do his best work. Furthermore, when final decisions are made concerning the program plans, either present or future, there is no one man who knows more about the problems and potentials of the people who make up the church membership than the man who devotes all his time to the every day working element in the church. Naturally, he knows more about the household itself and would be in the most enlightened position to contribute invaluable assistance to the elders by his participation in their business meetings.

Since intelligence, education, wisdom, and an influential mind are the preconditions of the eldership in employing a man to serve as their spiritual advisor, it is a lack of their own stability, by a contridiction of their own prerequisite requirements, when elders shut the preacher out of their business meetings. The denigration of individually insecure elders appears in a variety of verbal reasons for not including their preacher in the business meetings: There are misinformed elders who express their stupefaction with the words, "He doesn't belong in the business affairs of the church." A few fearfully insecure members of an eldership who feel that the preacher might attempt to "run the meeting!" Some elders seemingly have a passion for personal anonymity by not wanting the preacher's attendance in the business meetings. Elders cannot expect to get intelligent dedication to their program, responsive co-operation to the work, or even to keep a preacher's services for an indefinite time with this lack of expressed, confidential acceptance of him, regardless of his dedicated heart to the Lord's work. Such attitudes and expressions from elders are simply gross inconsideration of the preacher, and such individual remarks of unmitigated platitudes are unworthy of sound thinkers. Wise elders readily accept the preacher into their meetings, discussing the plans for their mutually shared hopes, ideals, and work with him. They will ask his advice on matters pertinent to their routine program, as well as future planning, and will listen respectfully to his suggestions. When his ideas are good ones, they will accept them as gratefully as when they are their own. If the preacher's recommendations are not considered workable ones, the elders will as graciously reject them as if they are from another elder.

Confusion can be prevented in the operation of a church program, as well as in the status of the preacher's work, when the elders discuss their future plans for any program changes with him in advance of a proposed routine change. For illustration, the experience of a preacher is related who was not given this just consideration and whose elders did not use righteous wisdom nor common courtesy in their inclusion of his being informed of their plans to change the program. This man was a diligent, conscientious minister who had rendered an invaluable service to his congregation for more than two years; years which had been made up of unhappy, sudden program changes. This persistent and fanatical practice of these elders excluding the preacher from their plans, denying him the foreknowledge of their program changes, affected this preacher's personal program to a frustrating extent. For instance, there were times when the elders would announce their alteration of the customary program for evening services for the benefit of having a visiting speaker who had been invited for the purpose of delivering a special lesson. While a guest speaker, with a special message, is good, the disregard for informing the employed preacher until the effective date was an inexcusable lack of consideration; he had spent the entire week in preparation for his lessons and sermons, only to have one of them canceled at the last hour. There is no humor, no justification, nothing but heartbreak in such working conditions for any man! The very center of emotional gravity in a preacher's work is rooted within a right relationship with his elders, just as his spiritual temperature is always being raised, or lowered, by the attitude of the eldership under which he operates since he is somewhat at the mercy of these men.

The judgment of a preacher who is new in a local service should be as wise in his caution for exercising diplomacy, in regard for time element, in becoming acquainted with the elders as he expects in reaching his cherished goal of earning confidential friendship with the other church members. A preacher should not expect to plunge into an immediate companionship with the elders any more than he should attempt to plunge headlong into the middle of their progressive business affairs. He will need time for carefully acquainting himself with both, the elders and their business operations, just as he will need consideration of time for the elders to become acquainted with his individual characteristics and abilities. When it is the blessed, good fortune of a preacher to serve under the working conditions of a considerate eldership who appreciates the vital importance of his participation in all aspects of the church business, materially as well as spiritually, he must realize his portion of responsibility in maintaining harmony. He should as solemnly and humbly accept the rejection of his proposed suggestions which are considered dissatisfactory by the elders as he gladly receives their acceptance of his approved ideas; he, too, is capable of fallible thinking and must guard against human error in reactions. The preacher is under the same obligation as his elders in measuring their respect one for the other, with the constant sense of appreciation for one another's position of responsibility in being faithful, tireless, appointed servants of the Lord. Each must share in the work of supervising in the Lord's church.

DISAGREEMENTS BETWEEN ELDERS AND PREACHERS

Human relations between preachers and elders may be termed equalitarian and, in this respect, their relationship should be neither preacher-dominated nor elder-dominated. However, as in all relationship, or business, of close human contact there will be a difference in opinions at times, but these occasional differences need not be harmful either to their harmonious unity or detrimental to their work. In fact, when human disagreements are recognized as the pre-rogative of personal thinking and discussed in the spirit of Christian-ity, with loving respect one for the other, such differences may prove to be helpful stimuli for greater growth. A genuine Christian atti-tude prevailing in the hearts of the elders and the preacher will be re-vealed at these times of a variance in human opinions, which can be a strengthening factor in their working relationship. As an illus-tration, one of our larger congregations, known for its activity, strength, and far reaching program of spreading the gospel of Christ, has the type elder-preacher relation which allows and shares a respect-ful difference in personal opinions occasionally. When the preacher of this church knows of some work which needs to be done in the pro-motion of a better program for more growth, he has the freedom of expression. If the eldership does not agree with his suggestions, or visualize the need for his proposal being put into immediate effect, this preacher with all due respect for their opinion pursues one of two courses of action: He either presents an appeal for his suggestion, with all the pros and cons necessary to convince his elders for the reasons justifying the proposal, or abides by their wisdom in rejecting the plan.

There is never any righteousness in the outcome of disagreements between elders and their preacher resulting in malicious resentful-ness, since infrequent differences in opinion are a result of normal, human minds and individual thinking. Extreme caution must always be exercised prayerfully, however, by all individual elders and preachers that un-Christian attitudes, betraying self-righteous feelings, will not develop from a friendly disagreement within their groups. Since all men are human beings there is the danger of malig-nancy being the ultimate reward for such pernicious attitudes and Christians are warned by the Lord to guard against having an evil disposition toward one another. Thus, frequent variances in human opinions, between elders and a preacher, can tend to be injurious to each person involved and indicative of uncharitable feelings among

them. There is an appreciable difference between a Christian difference in opinion and maleficent quarreling.

OPERATIONAL FREEDOM FOR THE PREACHER

The work of a minister is so diversified as to render incapable the
possibility of maintaining an hourly, or daily, established routine.
Wise are the elders who realize this fact and who put into practice
their expressed faith in the preacher by allowing him absolute operational freedom in his daily work. The eldership that invents an iron-
clad schedule for their preacher's office hours, his designated day to
be off, habitual time for personal calls and hospital visitation, is denying their expressions of belief in his diligence to the work for which
they have engaged him to perform, as well as refuting his power for
personal capabilities.

Preaching the gospel of Christ is the primary purpose of a
preacher's life, but this soul saving effort is not confined to the pulpit only; it is divided into the many channels of response to human
cries for help, with each one presenting a different form of opportunity. He stands, or falls, by his persuasive ability in the pulpit and
long hours for study in preparation for acceptable presentation of his
sermons are required. A local minister has the ever-present pre-
occupation with his individually required study, but these hours must
be arranged between the staggering bursts of odd-hour calls required
in the process of reflecting the mental, emotional, financial, parental,
and marital difficulties of the human relation problems that are ever
present among the church members and community citizens. When
someone has the need of the preacher for counseling, or he receives a
call from a hospital, or death of a loved one requires his presence
to console the bereaved and arrangements for the funeral needs attendance by him, an entire morning, full day, and perhaps half the night
may concel his pre-arranged schedule. Hence, common sense in the
best practical thinkers among the elders dictates the valuable necessity
of permitting the preacher all release from pressure by them, in any at-

tempt at disciplining his daily routine of work.

A loafing preacher is not to be tolerated and is not worthy of his hire, but dedicated servants of the Lord are seldom to be found loafing. When an occasional recuperation from a twenty-four hour vigil at the call of duty is required, a preacher cannot be accused of spending his time in idle loafing on account of inhabiting a human body, with the same physical limitations as other persons in pushing their bodies to extreme capacity and suffering exhaustion. While brethren are justified in condemning a preacher who would make a practice of wasting his time, there are instances when congregants, even elders, are guilty of aiding and abetting the preacher in time wasting by frequent invitations for coffee breaks. These persons often expect their preacher to halt whatever his pursuit of work, at any hour of the work day, to have a cup of coffee and banter some insignificant form of conversation. Some of these well meaning, but unthoughtful members, may even become personally offended if their minister refuses their invitation, unmindful of the many pressures against his time which their kind temptation often increases. An occasional respite from his desk will serve as a physical and mental refresher, but caution needs to be exercised in these coffee visits not becoming a habitual calamity for the preacher's schedule of work.

Elders who have retired from their occupations have been known to become offenders by encouraging time wasting, delaying and deterring their minister's work by frequent visits to his study. This creates a problem for the preacher in his effort to utilize capably the time for which he is employed and without wounding the pride of the retired elder. The offered suggestion, as the most practical way, for elders to improve the performance of a preacher is to leave him alone, trusting in his ability, honesty, and integrity for working out his individual schedule effactually and successfully. The proof of his diligent efforts will be self-evident in the finished product of his labor; neither a preacher's work not the fruits of his labor can be measured by a time clock.

THE IMPORTANCE OF STANDING TOGETHER

When an eldership and preacher are as one, in fiduciary unison they stand; when these men are divided in a lack of oneness, they will surely fall, causing an immeasurable injury to the church which they have pledged to serve. Despair, which lames many Christians and congregations, results often from the lack of confidential loyalty with-in the leadership of elder-preacher relations. An occasional word from a respresentative of the elder's group to the congregation, with respect to their minister's effort and approved labor, is both essential and spiritually healthy for all concerned.

A vitally important part of a local preacher's mission is the necessity for sermons which buffet and rebuke members of the Lord's church. While this type of lesson is painful to hear, it is no less painful to preach, but are commanded by God for the purpose of correcting the ills and strengthening the weaknesses within the household of the church. An eldership that is scriptural requires that these sermons be preached whenever needful, and yet too often the preacher is left to stand sadly alone insofar as the church inhabitants hearing words of commendation for his effort from their elders. For illustration there is an eldership, within a certain congregation, that has established a habitual practice of having one of their members add a few, but well chosen, remarks in behalf of their preacher; expressing wholehearted approval of his sermon and grief for the necessity of the rebuke because of some evident lack of harmony with God's law within the church. This is a congregation that is developing in Christian attributes while growing in numerical size; this is a church that knows the full measure of joy in the leadership of its elders who stand behind their preacher in his efforts and who stand for the principles their minister preaches. The members in this congregation have the happy assurance, from the past experience of their elders and preacher walking hand-in-hand through the ordeal of a large building program, that whether their future project is a budget expansion, increased gospel preaching project, or an old fashioned scriptural spanking, all is well because their leadership is expressed in a oneness.

The preacher of a congregation should be as conscious of a need for his expressed appreciation and consideration of the elders, in an audible word to the membership now and again, as the elders should be of him. Most elders live and die, in their untiring faithfulness of service, with very few words of gratitude issuing from the pulpit. The preacher would serve his elders and assembly well by preaching an occasional sermon to remind and exhort the membership of their individual duty to their elders. There are full grown, loyal subjects of Christ who are not fully aware of the scriptural obligation for their obedience to support all programs planned by their eldership. The minister is scripturally wise who will instruct and admonish the local membership, from time to time, concerning the solemnity of God's word with regard to their duty in respecting the elders who serve in overseeing its spiritual interest.

A preacher is foolish and unstable who will allow elders to be criticized in his presence; just as elders are equally guilty and lacking in wisdom who will permit criticism of their preacher, without both coming to the defense of one another. The often repeated adage of a wise man is appropriate for emphasis, "A dog that will bring a bone will carry a bone!" The very same person who will criticize an elder to a preacher will, with the same rapidity and disrespect, criticize the preacher to an elder. The leadership of a congregation who will countenance any unfavorable remarks, or discussion, of one another stands not together in the Christian spirit of oneness.

THE PREACHER'S SALARY

The salaried servant of the Lord is quite often the most abused Christian in a church, with his reimbursement the most neglected portion of a church budget. In fact, the very mention of the preacher's salary will stir up a paradox of emotional thoughts within the mind of an average, adult Christian, issuing forth in a variety of verbal expressions. The devout man, with a generous soul, who is well versed in scriptural admonishing for the preacher's adequate support will feel a twinge of chagrined distress when this subject is discussed. Yet when the economic question of the preacher's financial needs is raised, his embarrassed silence will be the denotation of his spriritual and moral lassitude. The denigration of such gruff remarks as, "A man shouldn't preach for money!" tumbles forth from the scripturally unenlightened minds, or miserly hearts, of some brethren. Often their covetousness will be exposed by insatiable demands for an overloading work schedule of the preacher and by their caustic statement, "That's what we pay the preacher to do!" When an eldership, or membership of a congregation, are guilty of such acts of misfeasance and uncharitable spoken words, they blacken their own hearts, condemn their own souls, and distress their Lord in being out of harmony with His expressed commands.

The existing condition of most preachers being paid an insufficient compensation for their hired wages is primarily due to the misapprehension, misconception, of unlearned minds by a lack of knowledge regarding God's instruction on this subject. The majority of sincere brethren use unsound thinking resulting from ignorance, rather than from miserly hearts, with regard to paying the preacher a proper salary. The following discussion of this controversial subject is an honest attempt to enlighten and clarify the distorted viewpoint of many Christians by giving some indisputable, factual information.

Sacred history, by exhortation and example, supports the practice for paying a preacher, but as to the amount there is no Divine specification. The Lord created man with a good mind, expecting him to use it, and it is a matter of common sense knowledge that an individual's expenditures rise to meet his work requirements. Thus, economy of the times, cost of living expense, numerical size of a congregation and its contributions, with the demands and requirements of a preacher's work should be the factors governing the amount of salary that he should receive. An eldership that uses the average salary of the congregants as a thumb-of-rule, for supposed "wise" thinking, in deciding the appropriation for their preacher's income is not exercising wisdom or good judgment. The ordinary living expense of a preacher would be comparable with the average church member, but his operating expenses will be considerably more than the average wage earners.

First, there is the item of his transportation which is recognized by the most conservative minds as being more costly that the automobile expenses of an average business man. A preacher's automobile will be driven from thirty to fifty thousand miles during the same period of time that the average member's car will be driven ten to twelve thousand miles. The mileage put on the minister's automobile will be used ninety percent in direct connection with his work in serving the congregation for which he labors. This wear and tear on his car will necessitate, over and above frequent minor repair services and purchase of new tires, the requirement for buying a new one more often than is ordinarily necessary for the average business man. Even with the best of care, if a preacher does not trade-in his automobiles within a reasonable time, the major expenses involved in keeping the old one repaired will become an excessive financial burden; in addition to this will be his mental burden for concern in not knowing whether or not he will reach a desired destination when enroute to a call for some given work. Most business firms who employ a man to do as much automobile work as that of a preacher furnish his employee with a company owned car, with the addition of an expense allowance to his salary that is based upon his mileage. Of course, it is neither a desirable nor practical custom for a church to afford their preacher's automobile. It is reasonable, however, that a congregation should understand the usage, which involves larger expenditures than the average amount, of their preacher's automobile.

The second, undeniable appeal for an above average salary is the necessity for a preacher's clothing expense being considerably more than the ordinary citizen's. Without being extravagant, the preacher must be better attired than the average workman since he is expected to be well dressed at all times, for the every-day work routine as well as for all unexpected demands made upon his personal appearance. The days are long past when a preacher needed only one suit for pulpit wear, funeral services, and hospital visiting. The time was when by public demand, he could wear a shirt, with or without tie, and trousers for his usual work day's attire; in some rural communities the wearing of overalls was considered fashionable and acceptable for the preacher's work dress. However, the present participation of most preachers in their church work and community programs requires them to wear clothing daily suitable for pulpit service. A congregation would be ashamed of a shabbily dressed preacher, with justification, since his appearance is a reflection upon the church supporting him for these physical needs. The upkeep of his wardrobe is no small item of expenditure when the expense of drycleaning, laundry, and garment replacement is considered. Members of a church would be shamefaced by their representative being a grease spotted, dirty collared individual! The church does not furnish its preacher his clothing as a "uniform" for working nor pay the costs of upkeep for his wardrobe as an addition to his salary, but the amount involved in these expenditures should be considered when his wage is decided.

While liberality in individual contribution is one of the most difficult lessons to preach for acceptability by a congregation, the preacher practices personal generosity for several reasons. First, he fully realizes the importance of his sermons being applicable to himself and that the core of individual love for God is centered in the act of personal liberality. Second, he is cognizant of his double responsibility for practicing what he preaches. Third, the preacher is expected by both the Lord and the church membership to be a living example of New Testament teachings. Thus, a preacher's personal contribution is often out of proportion with the salary paid to him by the congregation. The expectations for a preacher's generosity in contributing to outside sources, such as civic charities and almsgiving, is more mandatory than for the average Christian. Also, he is acutely aware of the Lord's words, "Inasmuch as ye have done it unto one of the least of these, ye have done it unto me."

There are some honest, but uninformed folk, who think that the monetary profits are great from such special services as weddings, lectures, and extra teaching programs for which a preacher receives token remunerations. When, in fact, the expenses totaled for his participation out-weigh the amounts paid to him; wedding gifts of his family, time and transportation cost involved for his participating in lectureships, are mentioned as only two of the reasons why the preacher seldom does more than break even financially. The entire sum received, in dollars and cents aside from the preacher's joy in performing these additional services, is usually barely enough to compensate for his personal expenses.

The general application for treatment of a preacher's salary is practiced by most congregations: Employ a man for a stipulated amount and it becomes his "fixed" salary for the duration of his service with that church; whether it be for one, or one hundred years! There are too few elderships who have arrived at the wise decision for reconsidering all salaries each year. While this does not denote the necessity for an annual increase, it does imply that these elders' minds are open in thinking, fair in consideration, for the possibility of raising any one of the paid employees salaries when such an increase is justified. The wage of each employee should be considered, discussed, and if the elders deem it advisable they will talk with anyone of these individuals concerning the sufficiency of his earnings.

An increase in the numerical size of a membership and in their monetary contributions should be determining factors for increasing the preacher's salary; such consideration is used to denote appreciation for an individual's worth in secular business firms. Sad but true, the same good sense in consideration of a preacher's worth is not understood nor applied as in other fields of endeavor. For illustration, there was a minister who had done an outstanding work in a particular church and he was appreciated by all its members. They were genuinely proud of their growth, as well as grateful for their preacher's meritorious effort in this achievement. When a visiting preacher was among them holding a meeting, he spoke on the subject of supporting a preacher in local work as the theme for one of his day sermons. On this occasion, the evangelist complimented the local preacher and membership upon their rapid growth, inquiring of an elder, who was sitting near the rostrum, as to the percentage of increase in their overall program when compared with previous year's records. The elder gave an enthusiastic, glowing report that both their attendance and contribution had doubled during the years that their present minister had been working with them. In answer to the next question as to whether or not their preacher's salary had been proportionately increased, the same good elder responded with a shamefaced, doleful negation. There was no prideful enthusiasm in this elder's realization of their failure to properly evaluate their preacher's worth to them by increasing his salary. Later in the day, another man who was a building contractor and one of the deacons for this church, made a truthful statement when he said, "We use much better judgment in our system of secular business ethics than we do in the Lord's business; for, if a man joined my firm who doubled my business income, I would gladly and readily double his personal salary." In sincere reply to the person who might ignorantly retaliate to this contractor's statement with the remark, "The preacher was not solely responsible for their increase!" it is suggested that he investigate the growth of a church which lacks the stimulation of an energetic preacher.

An eldership who will declare their fears of the congregation's refusal as their excuse for not increasing a deserving preacher's salary is lacking in two respects: First, such an unjustifiable, unsound act of reasoning is an indictment against these elders for their failure in teaching the congregants their scriptural duty and obligation to financially support the minister. Second, such utterances disclose the membership's disregard for their leadership and lack of respectful confidence in the eldership. A church is no different from other organizations with regard to the old adage, "A group is as strong, or as weak, as its leaders." When fearful elders try to compensate for an inadequate salary by hiding a given amount of money in secret slots, with such designations as "car expense," they insult the intelligence of the church membership and retard their spiritual development. The adult member of average mentality and intelligence can ascertain that all such hidden designations embrace the total amount of their preacher's income. Such so-called "extra allowance" will not benefit the preacher, but will cause financial grievance to him since he will be required to pay tax on the money which is secluded in the slot marked "car expense." The only additional amount which will benefit both the congregation and the preacher, enjoyed by them without the necessity for paying tax on it, is the church home expenses; this is a deduction allowable by the government. A church is permitted to furnish a home and pay the utilities for their preacher, tax free. It is the contention of learned Christians that members of the household of faith are ready and willing, when financially able, to increase their preacher's salary to meet the pressures of present-day economic conditions for the cost of living.

There is no provision made for preachers in sick benefits, or pensions, either by Holy writ or human code. Therefore, the sole means for human survival in either one of these needs is his ability to secure some personal savings for these purposes. The emergency of physical sickness and injuries will be as likely to occur in the lifetime of a preacher as for any other Christian family. When a man's salary is inadequate for him to secure a savings, or insurance plan, for meeting such possible emergencies, he is encumbered with a mental problem. For example, there was the case of a preacher who had preached and served the church faithfully for more than twenty years when physical difficulty developed, disabling him for work. When surgery was needful for the faulty condition of his vocal cords, which would cost several hundred dollars, he did not have the amount of money needed for meeting this expense. This minister was unable to preach for the many months while receiving medical treatment and during that time he became oppressed with insurmountable indebtedness. The sum of one hundred dollars was benevolently bestowed upon him by the congregation he was serving when stricken by physical disability. Such miscarriage of justice, miserly judgment in providing for the physical needs of one of His faithful servants, must surely grieve our Lord!

The soluble recommendation for the problem of properly paying' the preacher is to base his salary on the number of fifty-two weeks per year. While it cannot make any appreciable difference to the eldership, or other church members, that he receive his alloted salary in fifty-two weekly periods, it will be a differential wage to the preacher. In this manner of receiving his salary, he is able to earn the extra amount needful for those emergencies which arise with all human beings. This will eleminate the possiblity of financial losses and strain when he is away from home, holding a revival meeting for a church in another locale, also.

The dedication of a man's lifework to preaching the gospel of Christ, his devotion in serving the spiritual and human needs of a congregation, should not be decried on account of his physical needs for life's necessities being practical. A preacher may suffer intolerable hardships for his love of preaching Christ, but this love will not pay his grocery bill, clothe his back, or place a roof over his family. Dedicated churches of devout and intelligent Christians will begin their benevolent work at home by generosity in adequately supporting their preachers.

EVANGELIST AND LOCAL PREACHER

The purpose for a congregation's supporting a gospel meeting is to arouse the interest of community citizens, and to regenerate the spiritual consciousness within the church members. This purpose can best be served for all concerned, furthering the cause for Christ, when an evangelist is one with whom the local preacher can work in a spirit of harmonious compatibility. An eldership practices wisdom when plans are being formulated for a gospel meeting, with the names of preachers being considered, to consult with their local minister before extending an invitation to the guest preacher. The success, or failure, of the meeting effort depends extensively upon two elements: First, the evangelist and local preacher working together, combining their efforts for the duration of the meeting, will promote a greater influence and attendance. Second, the succeeding, or follow up, work which remains for the local minister to do after a meeting depends upon the efforts and type preaching done by the evangelist. When a visiting preacher is forgetful of his special mission purpose, desists from the gospel of Christ and begins to meddle in local problems of which he has heard, his sermons can do great harm. The local preacher can be left with the unpleasant difficulty of smoothing out the heedless remarks made by the evangelist, which work can consume weeks, or perhaps months, of his time.

The same truth is held as self-evident among the brotherhood of preachers as found in groups of other business colleagues. One preacher will be more likely to know first of any particular hobbyriding, or personality perculiarity of a fellow preacher, than the eldership. When the elders considerately include and consult with their preacher regarding the evangelist suggested for a meeting, he is in the position to disclose information which is his knowledge about the proposed man that could be injurious to the work for their congregation. A gospel meeting is one of the most important efforts undertaken by a church and sound thinking dictates the logic involved in the eldership and minister making plans pertinent to this work together. It is strongly suggested and urged that meetings be concerted endeavors at evangelism only, leaving local problems to be handled and solved by the local men. Unless otherwise specified, an evangelist is called for the purpose of preaching first principles of the gospel of Christ to a community; he should have proper respect for the work he is engaged to perform.

EVANGELIST'S REMUNERATION

There is a diverse need for the personality of a full time evangelist, but this makes him no less human in physical and material needs than the man who devotes all his energies to one congregation, preaching only occasionally in gospel meetings. However, in the remuneration for meetings of both categories of preachers, there are pertinent facts to be considered by the elders who are recipients as well as paymasters; whether or not all the preacher's efforts are devoted to preaching in gospel meetings. The very same truths are factual, as when considering the subject for paying a local minister, with respect to silence from the Inspired Word for a specific amount which would be proper remuneration for an evangelist. God intends and expects elders to use their common sense, knowledge of human expenses, combined with Christian generosity in this matter.

The time was when an evangelistic preacher received a larger remuneration for his service than the local preacher for his, but this has been reversed in present times until it has reached the point of absurdity in most churches and the existing condition is in need of a critical analysis. A preacher who gives full time to evangelism cannot adequately live, or often survive the cost of present day living expense, on his compensation for this type work unless he pushes himself to the inhuman effort of preaching every day in the year. This struggle for survival affords him no time for mental and physical recuperation, not to mention relaxation. Many of our evangelists are forced by their insufficiently paid wages to seek supplementary employment, or their wives commit themselves to public work in order to supplement their inadequate income. For example, one of our outstanding evangelistic preachers, who is dearly appreciated throughout the brotherhood, is suffering this hardship of inadequate compensation for his full time endeavor in preaching the gospel in meetings across the country. His wife must endure the burden of her husband's being under-paid by working outside her home to secure additional income. When this faithful man goes home, exhausted between meeting appointments, their family life is frustrated by the financial pressure which necessitates public work for his wife. This existing condition is deplorable, inexcusable, and without justification.

"Go ye into all the world and preach the gospel" is a Holy commandment, and there is a dire need for such work to be done and men capable of doing it. The financial expenditures are greater for an evangelist than for a local preacher for several reasons. The evangelist receives no fringe benefits, such as a church owned home furnished for his family, with the utility bills paid by a church. Living expenses are doubled when he is away from home, which is most of the time, considering that his family expenses are in one location while he eats and sleeps elsewhere. Transportation costs for an evangelist in traveling from one place to another locale are prevalent, whether he drives, flies, or swims! In all equitable consideration, the preacher devoted to evangelism should be payed a more substantial amount than the preacher devoted to congregational work and who is the recipient of fringe benefits. Whereas, more often brethren do not take into account these facts and an evangelistic preacher's indemnity is barely enough to cover his personal expenses, much less care for his family. Pathetically true is the fact that our larger, financially more able congregations are most often guilty of paying insufficient wages to their evangelists. This gross error can and should be corrected. The elders and preacher of each church should engage in a fact finding, unbiased analogy of their individual recourse for paying evangelistic preachers and come to an agreement for paying larger remunerations if there is evidence of need for rectification. For illustration, a certain eldership was discussing with their preacher the subject of compensation for an expected evangelist. The local minister informed the elders that he did not believe the amount which their group was paying was proper reimbursement to the men who preached in their meetings, or to the preachers whom they engaged when he was away holding meetings elsewhere. This declaration was followed by a needful discussion and agreement for increasing these salaries of the preachers who filled their pulpit by special appointments. During the course of their discussion, an elder asked the preacher how long he he had felt they were in error in this matter. When the preacher confessed, "For months!" the elder humbly replied, "You have been doing us a wrong by not bringing this to our attention for as long as you've realized we've needed to rectify this error." This known experience justifies the suggestion for other elderships discoursing with their preacher on this subject, in a critical analysis of the amount they pay to their evangelists and visiting preachers.

The special efforts employed in evangelism are spiritually healthy, soul refreshing, for both the visiting preacher and for the Christians for whom he does the preaching. They go to their "first love" for speaking and for hearing spoken the first principles of Christ again. The man who leaves his local program in order to preach for another congregation in an evangelistic meeting revives his listeners with fresh thoughts and receives renewed inspiration from them. However, too often the evangelist suffers financial loss from these meetings because of improper consideration by the eldership that has engaged him for this service.

For positive illustration of the financial facts involved in an eight day gospel meeting, which duration of time would involve two Sundays, these hypothetical figures are used: A preacher whose home congregation paid him one hundred, fifty dollars per week would deserve three hundred dollars for salary reimbursement in an eight day evangelistic program. Added to this allotted wage should be the additional amount for his transportation, which figure would depend upon the distance traveled, of course. For benefit of this illustration, the figure used for traveling expense is fifty dollars. Computing these two amounts, this one meeting would actually cost this preacher the sum of three hundred, fifty dollars. When, or if, he is paid the three hundred, fifty dollar indemnity, the eldership does not compensate him for his personal services which are required in preparation and presentation of sermons for their eight day meeting. While evangelistic work is done for the individual's love of preaching the gospel, such efforts always constitute more than the additional work of the meeting. His responsibility to the program of the home church continues to be felt by him, with such work as material to be written for weekly papers, waiting his return. The recognition and appreciation of the benefits reaped from the spiritual activity of evangelism justifies a substantial increase in the wages paid to the laborer by that church, in most cases. The preacher who serves in these successes should receive monetary expression of appreciation as well as verbal acknowledgment by the eldership engaging him, when and if a church is financially able to pay for his endeavor.

The positive and righteously approved course of action of an eldership, doing more than "mouthing" love for the Lord's worker, is to properly evaluate all the factual information regarding the expenses incurred by a preacher who leaves his home congregation to preach in their meeting. The eight day evangelistic service, used for exemplification, is comparable to two weeks duration in his loss of time from the work at home. In other words, unless the brethren who engage a preacher to conduct their meetings compensate him the monetary value of his time and personal efforts, in addition to actual indemnity, he would do better financially by staying at home. To the unthoughtful Christian who would say, "It has already been suggested that a preacher receive his salary in fifty-two week pay periods by the church he ministers unto regularly!" be scripturally reminded that each congregation has its own individual financial obligation. In answer to the tones expressed by a miserly heart. "Preaching the gospel of Christ should not be valued by monetization!" these truths are related: Preachers are genuinely dedicated men, with love for the Lord's work and not love for money their first purpose in life; if this were not so, they would employ their time and their training in some other field of work. In almost any other business requiring the equivalent in education and personal effort, a preacher could realize a larger salary than he receives from preaching the gospel of Christ. This undisputable fact and clear, cold logic is proof positive that a man did not enter the ministry for the purpose of earning lucrative wages. However, it is no less an undeniable fact of clear and sound thinkers that a preacher is human who, as a resident of this world, must accept calculated demands for every day living expenses. It is the responsibility of each eldership, within individual congregations, to give proper consideration combined with prayerful meditation for accurate evaluation of the great worth of evangelism and evangelistic preachers.

REQUESTING A PREACHER'S DEPARTURE

When there is an element of doubt about the answer to a congregation's problem involving a variance between the elders and preacher, or some few individual members being in disagreement, a sincere searching of hearts should be made by each Christian before laying the blame for guilt at the preacher's feet. Too often it is a practice of human tragedy to use the preacher as a scape goat. The truth in each particular situation is not to be found in the corridors of human minds nor in self-righteous opinions, but to trust in the instruction of Divine wisdom and integrity of the inspired word of God. In recognizing that all human beings share equality in faults and by exerting more loving appreciation for one another, with a stout conviction that harmony within the Lord's church must be placed above human variances, many incomprehensible disagreements will be erased.

If, however, after a sincere, prayerful, concentrated effort has been made on the part of all members for continuance of their work together, the preacher's personal characteristic traits prohibit a harmonious blending with the needs of that congregation, it is in the best interest of the Lord's work that he be replaced. An eldership realizing that such a change is necessary should be most considerate in handling the situation. Human difficulties and personalities of one congregation have jeopardized the future work of a preacher when, by using the Bible for their book of etiquette, self-indulgence can be overcome by the spirit of Christ dictating the actions of elders. Among other things required by God, elders need to be quick in apprehension, clear in discernment, and fitted to exercise their rule for decisions with magnanimous intelligence.

The first suggestion for handling a delicate situation as the action of dismissing a preacher is to practice the principles of the scriptures by discussing the problem with the preacher, with gravity, earnestness, and love. It is unfair for an eldership to practice laxity in the matter of informing a preacher of the reasons for his dismissal. Faults there are bound to be since by nature men are nearly all equal and when elders decide that it is in the best interest of their congregation to change ministers, they should tell the preacher why he is being replaced with all the gentleness possible. The   second   suggestion is that the elders give the man a reasonably sufficient period of time to find another place to work. During this time, the eldership should exert maximum effort in securing the service of another preacher, who will best serve their needs, so that the congregation will not suffer from the lack of a minister.

APPROPRIATE LENGTH OF MINISTRY

The appropriate length of time, as numbered in years, for a preacher to work with a church is a question misunderstood, with an answer misapplied. The duration of a minister's service in one location is neither given by commandment nor example in Holy instruction; thus, common sense is to be applied in designating the answer to this perplexing question. Most brethren do not use the same ordinary reasonable thinking relative to the length of time which their preacher should remain with them as they use with application to their secular business leader. As many years as a congregation is growing, developing, and working harmoniously together in their service to the Lord is just as many years which their preacher should remain with that church.

Many of the same human fallacies applicable to elders escaping their individual responsibility by firing a preacher are the ones which serve a preacher when he quits and moves away from a church. Such unwarranted, self-deceptive action is not following the path of righteousness, much less serving the best interest of the Lord's work. All Christians need to learn faithfulness, diligence, and reverent attention to the Lord's business as the best possible solution in determining the most appropriate duration for a preacher's ministry in one congregation. The faulty desire for frequent moves is often a preacher's personal refusal to accept some of the difficulties required in his staying with a church over a number of years. Remaining in one location for years demands more of his resourcefulness in study, variety of sermon presentations, patience and diplomacy in counseling the repetitious personal problems which is part of his work. The preacher who moves frequently from one church to another, for reasons of personal laziness in repeating the same sermons and inaptness to face reoccurring human weaknesses, is akin to the psychotic woman who changes club membership often in the desire to have her old hat admired by a new audience, or her instability for tolerating faults in old friendships.

All blame, of course, cannot be laid at the preacher's feet for his needing to move from some congregations. There are situations created by an eldership, or arising within the membership, that make his stay impossible. A preacher is vindicated for leaving a church that will not pay him a liveable salary, when the elders will not stand behind him in promoting their programs of work, and when the membership do not accord him proper human consideration. An example of such vindication is when the minister decides that it would be wise to move, for one of a dozen justifiable reasons, he talks with the elders about the advisability of leaving them and they give him no more encouragement than to say, "Well, we don't want you to move, but we don't want to stand in your way!" Such conversational inertia is an indication that these elders do not care enough for the Lord's work, this man, or his staying to investigate his reasons for leaving. These elders do not have enough concern for the welfare of the congregation, which is their obligation to oversee, to put forth the effort in trying to work out any problem which the preacher may have. When, in fact, the problem might lie in their laps, or be one that with deserved attention by them would avoid a change for church and preacher. The congregations and preachers who appreciate one another, respectfully continue to work together throughout passing years, have always experienced more harmony and enjoyed a depth of serenity which results in growth for themselves and the Lord.

Grievous is the fact that very often a preacher moves on to a new location just at the time when he and the congregation are prepared to do their best, most profitable work. There is no sensible reason for a preacher's not spending most of his service life in one place when he and a church are well adjusted and working happily together. The more years that a man stays in one location, the more influence he can have in the community of that church; the stronger both he and the congregation will grow in their influential worth to God. There is much comfort and great joy to be derived from teaching one generation, following in serving that generation's children; such a length of ministering service will instill greater confidence in all persons of the Christian relationship.

It is strongly advised that preachers cease to contemplate their worth to a church by the number of years that they have served and concentrate upon their labor by approaching new avenues of thought for better work in saving more souls in that location. It is just as strongly advisable for elders to give proper appreciation to their preachers by consideration of their physical, spiritual, and emotional needs in wholehearted support. Christians exert less energy in practicing human compassion by "quitting," or "firing," but the Lord admonishes us all to be "long-suffering toward one another." God will reward the fruits harvested by the combined efforts of all Christians, which are not reckoned by time as we count years.

CHAPTER III

ELDER-DEACON RELATIONS

The New Testament Law does not give explicit instruction for the work that is to be assigned to a deacon, but the obligation of his duty is implicit in the meaning of the word, "one who assists." Therefore, since the appointed work of an elder is clearly defined as being an "overseer," the deacon is scripturally designated to assist in the work of a church. The following association of ideas are discussed in an effort to comprehend and better understand the relationship between these brethren.

UNDER THE OVERSIGHT OF THE ELDERS

The men scripturally qualified as deacons are to serve in this capacity under the oversight of their elders. There is no specified time given for the duration of their service because the needs for this service are inexhaustible. The misconstrued idea that the elders are appointed to look after the spiritual affairs of a congregation while the deacons are to oversee the temporal management of business is erroneous and unsubstantiated by the Word of God. The elders have complete oversight of all work, including whatever assistance they may need from the deacons in their planned program. The reference to seven men who were appointed to wait tables in the Jerusalem church is sometimes used as a basis for limiting the work of deacons, but this is a miscomprehension of the true worth of these men. Some of these formulated opinions have been vague conceptions, more-than-less inherited, throughout the years and a closer examination is needful to properly evaluate the deacon's responsibility more accurately.

The minconstrued conception that deacons should have the oversight of temporal matters has created confusion in some congregations and provoked heartbreak for devout men. For a classic example of such an instance is to relate the position a deacon once filled, in a certain church, as "keeper of the purse." For several years this man served as overseer of the financial business in this congregation, making solitary and independent decisions in all sincere, good conscience that as an appointed deacon, he was scripturally fulfilling his duty. He was a spiritually humble man who was genuinely grieved upon learning that he was practicing an unscriptural position as financial manager and corrected his practiced error most willingly. Of course, the depth of grief in this situation was centered in the ignorance of the elders and their allowance of such practice for disbursing the money of the church. If this deacon had been less worthy as a devout and conscientious Christian, the congregation could have experienced unhappy confusion created by the willfulness of human nature.

In contrast to this example of a righteous deacon's action is the illustration of a group of deacons who acted involuntarily against the New Testament teaching in their refusal to abide by a decision of their elders. These deacons opposed the elders' decision to dismiss their preacher, reasoning that since they were responsible for overseeing material affairs of the church, they would continue payment of the minister's salary. With this thinking as their basis for action, and in all good conscience, these deacons openly opposed the decisive action of their eldership, creating a division in the church. While their unlearned thinking and unscriptural action is not to be condoned, the guilt of these deacons must be shared by those men who failed to teach them the truth of their relationship with the elders.

When men are appointed to serve as deacons, they should be instructed and fully understand that they are to work in the capacity of assistants under the direction, or oversight, of their elders, with no independent authority. In this decorous relationship, the value of deacons to their elders, congregation, and Lord, is inestimable. Their willing assistance can promote harmony for bigger work and better growth in the Lord's church.

JOINT MEETINGS OF ELDERS AND DEACONS

When deacons are appointed to serve in a congregation, it is advisable that a meeting be held for the purpose of the elders' familiarizing them with the current affairs of their program. During this meeting an elder, or the preacher, should acquaint these men with the importance of their appropriate obligation for serving under the eldership, at all times. Such a meeting at the beginning of their service, wherein a proper relationship between elders and deacons is clearly defined in a diplomatic declaration, will save future misunderstandings for the entire congregation.

There is great value to be derived from a monthly meeting of the elders and deacons for the purpose of discussing their program together. The ideas and suggestions from the deacons often prove to be invaluable to elders in their work progress; elders exercise wisdom who will treat suggestions of their deacons with respectful consideration. These joint meetings, however, should be for the purpose of discussing and assimilating ideas, not for the purpose of deciding a positive course of action. In a common sense approach to this subject, it is worthy of notice that in most congregations the number of deacons outweighs the number of elders and if joint meetings are held for the purpose of making decisions, a congregation can be overseen by the deacons rather than the prescribed elders. Joint meetings, between these two groups of men, serve an excellent reason for acquainting, or training, the deacons with the importance of the elder's responsibility, in which capacity they may one day serve. With regard to all final decision, agreements that are made by the system of vote in an elder's meeting, it is inadvisable as well as without scriptural foundation for the deacons to be included in the meetings of an eldership. Thus, caution should be discreetly used in the joint meetings of elders and deacons, so that all ultimate decisions will be deferred to the authority of an elder's meeting.

SEPARATE MEETINGS OF THE DEACONS

As to whether or not deacons should have meetings independent from their elders depends entirely upon whether such separate meetings are needful. When deacons have an appointment to do some specific work, such a special meeting might be necessary in order to expedite their particular assignment. For example an eldership requested that the deacons assume the responsibility for advertising an evangelistic meeting that had been planned. These elders instructed the deacons to stay within a fixed financial limitation, gave them a specified period of time in which to accomplish this work, and left all details for arrangement of this advertising program to the discretion of the deacons. In connection with their appointed work, these men needed to have several special meetings to colaborate in their specified task for division of the several means of advertising which were being utilized in the overall program. These separate meetings and the decisions made in these meetings were ones which affected only the special work appointed to them by their elders. When their program was successfully accomplished, with the work completed for this specific project, these meetings were no longer necessary and, thus, ceased.

SPECIFIC ASSIGNMENTS FOR DEACONS

There is no value or common sense in appointing a man to serve as a deacon when there is no work given to him for his personal achievement, just as there is no justification for having a large numerical group of deacons selected for "office" if they do nothing worthy of their appointment. It is spiritually healthy for both the church and individual deacon to be designated some appointed work in the congregation. Elders use wise discernment when they appoint deacons to specific assignment of service on certain committees, such as Building and Grounds Committee, Benevolent, Educational, Publicity, or some other particular portion of the program. Unfortunately, when deacons are appointed in some congregations, they are often only figureheads for several months, or even years, before being given any personal responsibility in the program of work. This is cheating the church which a deacon has been appointed to serve as well as the man, because his ability is left untapped when there is much work to be accomplished for which he may be qualified to render to the Lord's work.

PERSONAL QUALIFICATIONS OF DEACONS

In addition to the scriptural qualifications, set-forth by God, there are some required personal characteristics for the men who serve as deacons which need to be considered. These personal requirements are ones of human disposition that are formed by the habitual practices of a man in his secular business affairs and his relationship with other people. A deacon should be competent in his individual reliability, his dependability, and be a man who is trustworthy in keeping another's confidences. A man worthy of the appointment of deacon should be willing to give of himself unstintingly and faithfully to the work for which he has been selected. There are some individuals with the human fallacy of beginning well, but growing tired of the work he will finish poorly, or not at all. Men of this caliber will not render an adequate service to the church which they pledge to serve, but will only serve to make the elder's workload heavier. The man who is in need of being constantly prodded, pushed, or pulled in his effort of accomplishing an assigned work is childishly immature with the inability for qualifying in good character traits necessary for serving as a deacon. The type of personalities needed in this work are such as will help and not hinder the congregation's program by their individual slothfulness.

There are "dreamer" deacons who feel that their assignment in life is to dream up ideas for achievement by others. While it is an admitted fact that it takes dreams and ideas, there is no accomplishment unless these fragmentary pieces become a part of the whole plan by being concreted in action. Ideas and the man who has them have not the least value for attainment without achieving the goal by manual labors. This is applicable in the Lord's business, as in all other facets of life. Deacon should be living examples of men who can put good ideas to work, with constructive results by their personal endeavors. As one of the assistants to the elders, a deacon must be individually productive. The gospel cannot be preached, or souls saved, by wishing it were true; converting souls is a project demanding strenuously persistent progress.

SELECTION OF DEACONS

The spiritual and moral qualifications are clearly defined for a deacon, but the method for appointing these men is left to the common sense guide of the best adaptable arrangement in each congregation. The same question is provoked in appointing deacons, as in appointing additional elders, whether or not their selections should be made by the eldership and the same suggestions are applicable. The elders serving a church are in a more advantageous position to better know the men who would qualify in all respects of personality, but the final selection should be made by the congregation. It is advisable for the elders to consider the men who are scripturally qualified, selecting those who are best adjusted in personality characteristics for presentation to the membership of the church.

The self-same aspects are to be considered in carefully selecting men to serve as deacons, as presented for thoughtful attention regarding elder appointments. First, the elders are obligated to select men impartially, without the human pressures of good friends, family relations, or wifely solicitation. Second, the men whose names are selected for consideration by the elders should be individually contacted, prior to presentation to the congregation, to determine their willingness to accept this responsibility and to ascertain their attitudes toward the existing program. It is as important for the deacons to be harmoniously united in their support of the church program, both existing and future, as for the men who are considered for elders. After securing this information, the proposed names should be presented to the congregants, with a specified period of time allotted for their deliberation, before finalizing the appointments. If there should be personal objections from any member of the congregation to any man being considered for the office of deacon, such objections should be directed to the elders for a quiet and personal discussion. There might be a valid reason which would be acceptable as an objection for a man's appointment, and of which the elders should know. Again, it might be a point of personal misunderstanding, or misconception, on the part of the complainant which would need clarification.

When exercising caution in the important matter of selecting men to serve in the leadership of a church, Christians should act with warranted wisdom since there is no greater business in all God's created world than that of His ordained institution. Inattention, or unawareness, of the need for caution in deacon selection lets down the guard at the door of a church and very often allows disunity, strife, and dissention to enter; all such human error is condemned by God. There are some few instances when a man has sought the position of deacon, and even elder, for vainglorious reasons. Such men are not interested in the welfare of the church, but are as "empty vessels." When such an offender is discovered, the elders are under obligation to admonish and dismiss him before damage is done, either within their leaderhip group, or within the congregation. Elders cannot escape the consequences if they do not adjust, or eliminate, all causes resulting from the depravity of human nature that would create divisions within the Lord's house. A man who would seek an office, in the church for the purpose of self-elevation, rather than service to the Lord, is dishonest and unworthy to serve as a deacon.

DEACONS AND THEIR WIVES

A deacon needs the power of control over his tongue by not indulging in a rigmarole of conversation with his wife concerning the church business that is not to be disclosed for public information. He should cultivate the same care for her welfare as an elder for his wife, insomuch as the intricacies of the church affairs are concerned. A deacon's wife should not be depressed, or weighted down, with the burden of problems that sometimes make up the human element in the duties of her husband's work relation with the church leadership. She should not be incumbered with the fear of betraying some information confided to her, when this information is not generally known because it is best for the church that it not be divulged.

One of the requirements for personal strength of character, when a man accepts the duties of a deacon, is to share the burdens of the Lord's work in such spirit that there will prevail a state of harmony; individually according such behaviour as contributes to the well-being of all the saints, including his own wife. There is some information that is discussed within the confines of a joint elder and deacon meeting which should never be mentioned, or questioned, outside this group. Discourses from one of these meetings are not good topics for supper table conversation, and a deacon should be careful that church business not become church gossip! Certain matters of business, discussed by the leadership of the Lord's church, should be kept confidential by deacons and even excluding the knowledge of their wives when it is in the best interest of the congregation they serve.

ASSISTANTS OF ELDERS

No earthly joy is comparable to that experienced by a right relationship between elders and deacons. From the original meaning of the word the deacons are assistants to their elders, subordinates to these "overseers" in God's designed plan for their operation. In full connotation of the meaning given to this subordinate position is to understand the implication of the word in being submissive to the elder's authority. With their understanding acceptance of serving as obedient assistants to the elders, deacons can be of invaluable worth to the eldership, as well as to the church, in numerous ways. Many times the deacons are in a better position to learn of problems of which the elders are unaware, because persons will feel more at ease in talking with them than with elders, or the preacher. Individual members will more often express themselves freely to a deacon regarding some plan, idea, or need for the church program than to an elder. When such information is received by a deacon, he is in a position to disclose this suggestion to the elders, which can benefit their program. The confidences exchanged between elders and deacons affords immeasurably better understanding for their finite minds in doing greater work for the Lord.

The deacons must have an abiding respect for the elders, as so must the elders have for their deacons, in sharing a mutually advantageous joy in their working relationship. Rapport, or being a part of the singleness found in their united effort of serving the Lord, is the fundamental connection between elders and deacons. Without this oneness, there is not that flow of feeling absolutely essential to achievement in their common endeavor. The Bible teaches that worthy elders should be honored by all members of the church, and when deacons esteem these men, they are in harmonious keeping with the Lord's Will. In this spirit of willingness to be of the most possible assistance to their elders, the deacons will take a delight in their tasks assigned to them.

When their interest is deep, concern vital, respectful appreciation for the elders heartfelt, the deacons will be champions for their elders and for the decisions made by them. They will no more think of speaking critically about the elders than they will allow someone else to criticize these men in their presence. This Christian caliber will produce and preserve the capacity of mind that is personification of all a deacon should be in the sight of the Lord, and as a noble assistant to his elders.

DEACONS NEED ENCOURAGEMENT

There are no master and slaves, no straw bosses, in the churches of Christ. It is that system of organization in which God is the center of life, center of combined human interest, with the elders and deacons sharing the responsibility of directing this interest for upbuilding and glorifying God. The recognition accorded these men is not one of exalted position of reverence, but respectful compliance with their God given authority as shepherds and shepherd's helpers. Deacons are the men chosen for their several qualifications and abilities to serve as helpers in the work ordained for their elders, as "shepherds of the flock." Deacons, too, are to be respected for their selfless efforts in serving the Lord's church, they will have their share in the glory of the outcome of faithful perseverance, on earth and in heaven.

While deacons are a part of this great team of church leadership, they are individually human beings who often are in need of encouragement and commendation. They need expressions of gratitude for their untiring efforts in diligently serving as the elder's assistants, by the men they serve and by the members for whom they serve. Expressed appreciation will give them inspiration for continued effort, as well as satisfaction for tasks well done. A deacon is a man, like any other human being in the congregation, who can become discouraged "in" the work, though not tired "of" the work. He can die in his enthusiasm for the work, the same as anyone else, for lack of an occasional word of praise from the elders whom he assists. Bound together as they should be with strong cords of unselfish, loving respect, and appreciation one for the other, their gain in Godliness will be great.

CHAPTER IV

ELDER-CONGREGATION RELATIONS

The application intended in God's instruction that elders should be the overseers in the church does not confer upon these men the perrogative of dictatorship. Peter said that elders are not to be "lords over God's heritage", but are to be "examples to the flock." The relationship between elders and congregation is sometimes misconstrued, by either one of these groups, to such an extent that happiness is replaced by resentment, creating problems that hinder the Lord's work. For a better understanding of the scriptural application, regarding elder's proper relationship with a congregation, some subjects are discussed with proposed suggestions for deliverance from a few popular delusions. The work of a church is not done by magic control of the leadership any more than it is successfully accomplished under an autocratic iron hand, or demanded obedience to the eldership by these men. Christ is the autocrat of His church and every Christian in the congregation has work to do. Everyone must do well the work that is his assignment if he would be approved by God. "Workers together with Him", in a spirit of sympathetic compassion, will create understanding, happiness, and a respectful communication.

ELDERS ARE EXAMPLES

The elders of a church are to lead in all phases of their work by deed, as well as word, not by command. Great talkers are not neccessarily prolific doers and the best teachers are the elders who teach by their faithful actions, rather than dogmatize. Elders should be examples to their congregation in their faithful attendance to all services, or they belie their own words and refute their own plans for the church program. For illustration is the related instance where elders had spent hours in planning for a gospel meeting, and hours of talkative insistance for its support by wholehearted membership participation. Yet, their much talking was betrayed by their lack of support in personal attendance when few of the elders attended more than one or two services of the entire meeting. Such loud speaking is a sign of vanity when unsupported by concrete evidence of belief in action. There are congregations where an elder does not attend any service of the church he serves except on Sunday, and sometimes then he is present only for the morning hour of worship. This man cannot stimulate spiritual activity, inspire others, awaken interest, kindle enthusiasm, encourage learning and support of the program when he is absent. He is personified in the story of a man who rushed up to another fellow, standing in front of a country store, and asked, "Did you see a group of people going down this road?" When his inquiry was answered, "Yes, they went by here about an hour ago," he nervously replied, "Oh, my! I must hurry and catch them, I'm their leader!"

The measure of an elder's attitude toward the church program is best expressed by his individual participation and personal service rendered to God, since his highest function is his own faithfulness. His reverence and attention during the assembly services will be in harmony with the scriptures, as well as serve effectively in leading others to imitate his pattern for worship. A congregation whose elders roam around in the foyer, halls, or back-and-forth in the aisles throughout the duration of solemnity which should prevail for worshipping the Lord, are practicing duplicity. While standing outside the auditorium in the foyer, talking with one another and with tardy members, they are tantalizing misconduct among some members, hindering the worshipful attitude of others. Such misconduct is inexcusably distracting to the preacher who is doing his best to preach the Word of God to those who have a thirst for learning. The irreverence of attitude towards the service is insulting to the Lord, disturbing to those gathered for worship, and a practice of self-deception on the elder's part because he is leading others astray. The progressive course of an elder's habitual prancing around during the worship hour ends in serious departure from the reality of serving the Lord, which is the worst affront of the elder who indulges in an irreverent attitude.

Generosity exemplified by the elders is the most practical method for teaching a congregation liberality in their personal contributions. A church cannot be persuaded to be liberal if those who are the leaders cannot show forth the example of enlarged spirits in their individual practice. The failure of elders to cleave to the purpose deemed right in God's Holy Word is the worst of all failures, and a man should not be appointed to serve as an elder who refuses to be bountiful in his own purposed giving. An elder who is stingy with his money cannot encourage others toward liberality and is, in fact, a stumbling block to those whom he is charged to lead.

The advisement for a congregation being taught to purpose its giving is strongly exhorted: First because it is scriptural, and second because it is the best method for accomplishing great work for the Lord, with decency and good order. A church membership need not possess great wealth in order to be generous, for it is not the quantity, but the quality of the spirit in which Christians give that is reckoned by the Lord. The widow's mite is our example of approved generosity in understanding that God loves a cheerful giver. When the lesson for "purposed" giving is properly taught and if the elder's financial program includes the usage of purpose cards, these men should be the first ones to sign their cards. The best sermon preached on liberality becomes the most effectual lesson by a good example being set in the personal response of those men directing the affairs of a church. A worthy elder is a generous Christian who justifies his principles and the program he plans, by individual practice.

ELDERS SHOULD BE VISITANTS

The numerical size of a congregation is not a valid reason for elders not knowing their people, though often used as a flimsy excuse by some men for their personal indolence. A church that has a good, consistent visitation program which is led in practice by its elders, is a strong, growing, and working congregation. There is no better method for getting to know, know about, and for being known than for the elders to visit with members in their homes. Elders who are baffled by ignorance when seeking to promote some particular work in the church which calls for the help of a special talent from among their membership, can find relief from this ignorance by getting to know the church members. Visiting in the homes of their members will serve to learn more about their people individually, enabling the elders to help and to be helped whenever needs arise, in any given circumstance.

The men who serve as leaders for a church should be examples in their personal endeavors of their visiting program, as well as assuming the responsibility for instigating the plan for this work. There are elders who feel that since they do the "directing", their obligation for doing personal visiting is relieved. Factually, this is unscriptural. Even though a Christian is engaged in a special work of the church, as men appointed to an eldership, they are not released from the obligatory commandments of God's Word for personal participation in other necessary good works. The lethargy expressed by individuals suffering from spiritual listless disinclination is often proclaimed in such words, "We hire the preacher to do our visiting." Such an expression of mental and physical inertia is as justified as "hiring" the preacher to take the Lord's supper for another person! The preacher hired for assuming an elder's personal responsibility to any phase of their program is hired for the wrong purpose, which both common sense thinking and scripture dictates to anyone of average mentality. While the preacher is committed to do all the visiting he can with members of the congregation, he can no more fulfill this obligation for the elders than he can for any other personal obligation, of any other Christian. Words expressing such thoughts from an elder are indicitive of an attitude of languor of heart toward God, forgetful of the scriptural injunction, "Watch thou in all things."

The suggestion is made for the establishment, or continued practice, of a systematic arrangement in a church program whereby the individual elders would visit certain members each week. Common sense knowledge informs us that the Lord did not intend that the impossible should be attempted, as each elder visiting in all the member's homes weekly, monthly, or even yearly. However, over a period of time all homes could be visited by one member of the elder's group when a system for visitation is employed. There are some elders who have served as overseers in a congregation for years without having visited with anyone of their members, except for a few personal friends and family members. The success of an established visiting program is largely dependent upon the attentive, eager outlook that challenges energetic participation by those elders who plan the promotion of this work. For illustration the old story is related, "For want of a nail, the horse threw a shoe; for want of a shoe, the horse could not carry its rider; for want of a rider, the battle was lost; because the battle was lost, the kingdom fell; all because of laxness in driving a nail."

HANDLING PROBLEMS

Churches are composed of Christians who are human beings, with individual and collective problems. When a congregation lives harmoniously with few publicly known problems, it is not because none have existed, but evidence of the leadership of elders who are capable of solving such problems, quietly and efficiently. Guidance, correction, and discipline are a fundamental responsibility of the elders, outlined as a portion of their work by the Lord. It is their obligation to discharge the administration of whatever is needful in the best interest of the church to maintain right standards and relationships among the congregants. The problems within a church membership are as varied as human nature itself, requiring human tact combined with prayerful meditation for wisdom by the elders handling these problems.

An elder is not required to be a human relations expert nor psychoanalyst in order to have people seek his advice and help. He needs only to be genuinely interested in helping others, self-contained in his ability to keep sheltered another's confidence, and thereby proving himself to be trustworthy as a counselor. When a man accepts the responsibility of an elder, he should be attentive to learning whatever he does not know about human problems, of various nature, that he can better understand these human ills. The more he knows about the variety of illimitable difficulties that plague humanity, the better able he will be to alleviate these woes when encountered. When an elder does not have the time to help people with their human problems, he does not have time to serve as an elder! The elder who can be guide, refuge, and lend his strength in helping suffering souls with their human frailties is of invaluable worth to his Lord, whom he serves; his preacher, with whom he works; and his congregants, whom he oversees. It is unfortunate more elders do not inspire confidence of other people that is necessary for handling the flood of human ills that prevails amid Christians within their congregations, which would relieve the preacher of the necessity for doing most of this work. Wealthy is the church which has elders capable of being helpmates with the preacher in the bitter hours of trial that come into the experience of humanity composing the church inhabitants.

Individual problems, having to do with the personal nature of people's afflictions, requires that utmost confidence be maintained by the elder who is consulted. When members of a church have absolute confidence in an elder, they will not hesitate to counsel with him. If an elder discusses these delicate personal problems and frustrations with his immediate family, or close friends, he betrays an individual's trust, burdens his family with secrecy, and does harm within the Lord's church by losing the confidence of several Christians. For illustration, there was such betrayal in the particular case of a woman who discussed her personal heartbreaking problem with an elder. He broke faith with her, as well as the trust of his office, by relating her story at home. Within a few days, the children of the elder were spreading this woman's difficulty within the circle of church society, making it common knowledge for idle conversation. Without malicious intent, this lack of confidence in an elder's indiscretion, created grief and disappointment for many souls, including himself. This example of thoughtless misconduct is a common cause for rifts and divisions in congregations. Thus, it behooves all elders to exercise extreme caution, using discreet conversation, when they are the recipients of confidential information, involving the misery of someone's life, lest they become practitioners of idle gossip unintentionally.

There are instances when elders and preachers have problems that are discussed, which are in the nature of a human disagreement, that should be reconciled between themselves in a manner of confidential quietness; never mentioned outside the quarters of their meeting together. When mutual love, co-operation, and respect prevail among the leadership there is no quarreling, bickering, or resentment following their reconciliation, but it is in the best interest of their work that these variances not be aired in public. These leaders must always be ready, willing, and able to put the best interest of the Lord's church first in mastering, second by keeping publicly quiet, these clashes of personalities, or human opinions. Elders and preachers cannot ably oversee the work of a church who cannot conquer, or, master, their own human passions; always keeping in obedience their judgment in conscientious harmony with God's law for unity. The real test and the secret of self-mastery is for elders to fully comprehend the fact that human beings will come and go, but the church remains forever.

OBTAINING RESPECT FOR THEMSELVES

When the members of a church do not have proper respect for an elder, it is possible that the elder carries the blame and should indulge in self-examination. "Let the man examine himself," is the exhortation of the scriptures, and such an examination can be instructive, often correcting the cause for a condition of disrespect from other human beings; especially in a leader of the church. Elders should cultivate the principles of scriptural relationship with their flock by graciousness in action, characterized by genuine selflessness. This will not manifest weakness, but will reward them with loving respect instilled within the attitude of others toward them, by their example of Christian charity.

Elders must be examples of the principles for which they stand in their individual business pursuits. If an elder is not wholly honest, just, and upright in his secular business relations, not only will he be unable to effectively lead Christians, he will be a stumbling block to those persons within and without the church with whom he associates. Fortunately, the cases are few, but there are instances when an elder leads souls away from God, Christians astray, by his duplicity in business transactions. Honesty taught by word of mouth must be combined with integrity practiced in all human relations of an elder's personal life.

An elder's avowed purpose in serving Christ must be proven by his actions in the participation of community social life. The moral qualifications, set forth in the New Testament, for a man's eligibility in becoming an elder is the ruling guide by which he must conduct his social behavior as an elder. If an elder chooses unwholesome associates and social functions, accompanies gamblers, swearers, alcoholic indulgers, he cannot continue serving as a leader in the church. Even though he is not a partaker of these corrupt practices of society, his habitual presence with such persons will condone them and their activities. He will cast a shadow upon the church, lead souls astray, and eventually deceive himself into becoming a victim of his associate's gratifications.

The elder who does not have a right relationship within his home can lose the respect of church members. When he is without the respectful obedience of his children, permitting the wishes and whims of his children to govern his household, he will lose the respectful attitude of the congregants whom he oversees. When an elder cannot maintain harmonious control over his own dominion, there is no escape from the stern reality that he will be lacking in some attribute of character which would most likely affect his leadership in a congregation.

An attitude of respect from other persons is an earned emotion, not one bestowed with a title. An elder beloved and respected is a man who is open-minded, not obstinate in his own self-righteousness toward other people. When an elder is closed in his thinking, rejecting the ideas and suggestions of others for better ways to be considered in operating the church program, he is opinionated; without justification in expecting the respect that is scripturally due him from his fellow Christians. Growth and development of a congregation depends largely upon the open-mindedness of its elders, since men of this caliber will have the mental ability to swing into a bigger and better program whenever an opportunity is presented for their consideration. An elder needs to be of strong will in his character, but not stubborn in attitude. He must be able to crystalize his decisions in deeds, with determination in his actions, but capable of giving in to persuasive reasoning. Praiseworthy and honorable is the elder who is willing to consider views that are opposed to his own, when they contribute to spiritual development and numerical growth, while able to hold a scriptural course in planning the work of a church. Respect gained comes from respect given by an individual elder.

PLANNING FOR CONGREGATIONAL DEVELOPMENT

Thoughts for development are the beginning point for growth, the seeds of mental power engender planning for work which will be accomplished years later. The upward direction of a congregation's growth is determined by the expressed faith of elder's plans including the future, not by repression of thinking for their present, or current, needs only. One primary reason for the capacity of increased development of a church, or for its retardation and decay, lies within the unwavering purpose for continual growth that allows for no lapses. During the planning for expansion in errecting a new building, there is no triumph in the remark, "We will fill this building when it is completed, and that is as large as we need." This verbal expression of mental satisfaction echoes from the pathos of human inability to comprehend the inexhaustable plan for growth, as outlined by God in the Bible; beginning as far back as His promise to Abraham. When elders are lacking in foresight, unmindful of the fact that adequacy for present needs is not substantial for future growth, their inhibited thinking produces paralysis in active development. The example of three congregations engaged in their individual building programs, while this book is being written, with edifice plans that will serve only the current needs of their memberships, without producing the efficiency for future growth, is mentioned for factual proof of inadequacy. In each one of these respective building programs, the completed construction will accommodate their present membership needs, relieving the pressure of discomfort which brought about their new buildings, but within months of normal expected growth they will again be cramped for space and restricted for growth. This same lack of looking to the future is a grave mistake being made by elders in churches across the nation. To serve well our day and present generation is not worth-while activity in objectivity. Elders must cultivate perseverance and optimism in their planning for future development, if success for growth of the Lord's church is to be attained, and approved by God.

There are elders who thoughtfully plan adequate auditoriums, but who utterly fail to be as thoughtful in planning for the Bible school training program. The development of an active Bible study program, for various age group classes, is as important in the work of a congregation as the auditorium service, insofar as instructing humanity with a better knowledge of God's Word. There is no justification for elders being unmindful of the needs for adequate facilities in their Bible school program. Inattention to the requirements for this phase of the Lord's work can greatly hinder the over-all development of a church program. As children are trained from infancy, so will they grow into useful, or negligent, Christian adults and part of this responsibility lies in the Bible training they receive in the congregation where they are reared. Thus, it is vital for elders to afford the best possible equipment and building facilities in their planning. Competent programs will include planning for every segment of the various departments into which the work of a church is divided, materially as well as spiritually. In this generation of commodious aids, available for usage in teaching and learning, there can be no righteous reason for elder's failing to furnish the best materials possible for Bible teachers and students.

Wisdom in future planning for growth and expansion is in harmony with God's design, as well as common sense thinking for financial economy. An illustration of elders with vision in looking toward the future is exemplified in one eldership planning their extension of work for twenty years ahead of their generation. The congregation they oversee is one of the most rapidly growing memberships in the brotherhood, having reached its present numerical size within a short span of time. It is not by magic nor miracle that within ten years this church has accomplished more in good works than most congregations attain in a hundred years. Their present attainment are the fruition of plans made and goals set years ago, toward which they have worked with constant perseverance. The plans of this eldership for their future years' development would make some elders swoon in dizzy weariness, or skepticism, but faith in their future achievements being fully realized is based upon the solidity of their past record. The wonderment of such marvelous planning for the future years lies in the surrender of self-glory, since these elders will not live to witness the fruit of their work, most likely, but others will reap the reward of accomplishment in the plans they have made. The plans of these wise men will long outlive their individual years on earth, but they will reap the reward for their confidence of faith in the future of the church in that sphere beyond this world.

There is no less need for the internal, or spiritual, future development of a church than there is a crying need for longer range planning for materially housing a congregation. The physical substance of a well planned building can serve no better than the internal purpose for which it is intended. Elders should have an activated program for training future preachers from among their young men and teenage boys. Preachers for the future church must be made within the congregations wherein they are reared; Christian schools cannot do it all. While Christian colleges serve the higher echelon for training these young men in preparation for the ministry, elders should encourage their own to preach before they reach higher school level. There should be a planned and well executed program for teacher training service, also, avoiding the possibility for having a shortage of well trained teachers for Bible classes. When elders plan a teacher's training class in their program, they will inspire and instruct Christians in the highest capacity for Bible teaching and produce greater individual work in their congregation. While an annual series of classes on the subject, "Training for Service", is spiritually healthy, even better is a continuous operation of this type of class throughout the year. Bible teachers should be given every advantage and assistance for helping them to do better work, by developing their individual attributes in assimilating ideas from others; which can be the product of elders promoting a teacher training plan in their programing.

A special class designed for instructing new converts is needed in the program of work planned by elders. Inclusive in this class plan should be a personal visit in the new convert's home by one of the elders. It is a fallacy of most congregations to neglect the particular needs of a soul who is obedient to first principles of the gospel by not feeding their thirst for knowledge with the "milk" of scriptural enlightenment. The New Testament recognizes the need for this type teaching and personal work. The slogan, "Convert all you can; train all you convert; use all you train!" should be a principle foundation in the program of classes in all congregations. It is a pathetic fact that too often new converts are lost to the church, perhaps souls doomed throughout eternity, because of a lack of attention to their personal needs in being "new babes in Christ." When such is true, it is a serious indictment against the elders who are responsible, by neglecting to plan for the spiritual growth of new converts in their program of work.

An effective plan for evangelizing the community in which a church is located is a fundamental obligation of the eldership planning the program. Mission work is too often mentally catalogued as belonging to a foreign field, another city, or in some other state from where a congregation is based. When elders have the satisfied feeling that they are taking the gospel to the world by supporting, or co-operating in the support, of some work elsewhere, but are making no provision for effort within their home program to teach the local citizenry, they are deluding themselves with the despicable deceit of human nature. The steppingstone for spreading the gospel throughout the entire world is begun on the doorstep of each congregation. When evangelism is begun at home, it will stimulate fruitful activity towards being farther reaching then the elders dare to dream. The methods suggested for practicing this "doorstep" evangelism are by means of using the mediums of radio and television communications. Also, by affording printed tracts for disbursement by the individual Christians composing the congregation's member ship.

Elders of the churches of Christ have the charge from God and challenge of a needful world, for planning not only adequate programs for the current needs of their respective congregations, but for the development of future generations yet unborn. A church can accomplish no more than is planned for them by the elders who direct and lead their work. While it has been done, it is difficult for a congregation to rise above, or go beyond, its leadership. Furthermore, such action is out of harmony with the Lord's plan that elders are to be men capable of leading the programs and growth of the church they serve. The primary reason for a congregation being "fenced in", with respect to growth, is when its elders live on a plane of mental reservation, limiting their work by restriction in their thinking power beyond the present age. Blessed is the church with leadership composed of men with vision, because "Where there is no vision, the people perish." The satisfaction of attainments in the Lord's work could never be achieved without elders of wisdom who foresee the significance in long range planning, towards years ahead in their thinking of future development. The criterion to determine the quality of elder's understanding in the Lord's plan of their overseeing His work on earth, in a competent manner, is evidenced in their programs for future accomplishments, as well as in their efficient management of a congregation's current affairs.

CONFIDING IN THE CONGREGATION

Elders do not live in one partition of the church, while the congregants inhabit another portion; together they make up the organization of human society in which God is their mutual interest. While a congregation is under the direction of the elder's leadership, these men do not possess solely the wisdom of all the members nor power of thought that is found in collective thinkers. There have been instances when elders erroneously kept plans hidden, because of their misconception in thinking that the membership would not approve some particular plan. Most often, these men were laboring under false illusions, and by submitting their plans properly the power of new life would have been given these ideas by the combined force of the congregation's adoption. With but few exceptions, the members of a church are enthusiastically willing to support the plans for all programs of their leadership. In fact, they look to their elders for guidance in undertaking their individual places in the work of the congregation, where they serve and worship the Lord. More confidence and less fear would assist most elderships in a better discern-

,ment, with wiser understanding, for their position of responsibility in being looked to by their people in leading the work assignment for the church.

There is no advantage in the elders keeping secret any information that will ultimately affect the entire membership, or plans which they expect the members to support. When there is a building expansion program, the members need to be informed as to full particulars involved, from the onset of the elder's planning. When a new preacher is employed, the congregants should know that he is receiving adequate remuneration. If a congregation is engaged in a mission program, or some form of benevolent work, the membership is entitled to know how much of the financial budget is disbursed for this work, in what locations their aid is sent, and the results of the overall endeavor. Periodical information concerning the good works of a church should be shared with the entire membership, because with few exceptions they are individually interested. The elders should be as considerate in affording the membership an analysis of the work being planned and results attained, as they are in expecting participation, by wholehearted support, from the entire congregation. It is essential for the success of their working together, in any field of their joint endeavor, for elders to have confidence in the ability of their membership sharing their plans for the church program.

When there is an objection to some plan of action, elders use wisdom in discussing it with the conscientious objector. If the plan is worth adopting, it is worth defending! A program of work undertaken in the light of complete harmony, with co-operation by all members, can be performed with a balanced and firm confidence, resulting in greater achievement. If it is a rare case where some member expresses an unfounded objection, which the elders cannot dissipate with the consideration of individual explanation, the strength of self-confidence is tested and proven when their work is continued. United the elders and deacons must stand, without one dissentor among their group, when meeting the obstacle of a self-righteous objector who would stand in the path to block their worthy work being accomplished. For example, there was one man in a certain church who was allowed to hinder the course of action when a plan did not meet with his personal approval. Not infrequently, this man's objections over-ruled the elders' decisions in their proposed plans for the congregation's program. He was an outstanding, out-spoken, citizen of the community who was liberal in his financial contribution to the church. His dissenting voice alone could determine the entire course of action within the congregation. This man was unscriptural, and even worse, the eldership was unscriptural in their allowance of this one member to control the reins of operation for their program. He was a misinformed, misguided Christian whose burden of guilt was equally shared by misgovernment of the elders. Fortunately, a conscientious fellow-Christian cared enough about the progress of the Lord's work, and the misapplication of his influence, to diplomatically explain the man's error to him. While no man knows enough to pass judgment upon himself, with the spiritual aid of a brother he understood, judged himself guilty, and corrected his habitual objections for a constructive manner of action. This man's influence was put to good and scriptural usage in supporting the elder's future plans for development in the church.

Elders should not place limitations upon the membership by refusing to share their plans for all the work they hope to accomplish. There is unity, harmony, and a larger measure of success to be expected from the essential element of sharing all aspects of the work together. Elders advance in knowledge, as well as attain full support, when they confide their plans for the program of work to the membership. In all earth's places, there is no force which can withstand the impact of a united congregation working together in preaching the gospel, and serving their Lord through attending the needs of humanity.

THINGS TO AVOID

Elders are human and should be permitted to enjoy the same

preference for choosing their associations with other individuals whose personalities afford pleasant social companionship. However, in their capacity of serving as elders, these men need to avoid party groups which would exercise pressures of friendship, affecting their work of leadership. Elders must be cautious of becoming members of a clique within their congregation, if such cliquishness would produce harmful results in their work. The interest of an elder must belong to the entire church membership, where he serves, unbiased in attitude to his bipartisan relationship in elder-congregation association. His wholehearted concern must be the welfare of the church, for which he serves, and fidelity to the eldership, wherein he labors.

Political romances are sometimes courted by members of a church, and elders need to be aware of the danger of such courtships in order to avoid such entanglements. Sometimes an elder feels complimented by the attention of an individual member singling him out, time and time again, for consultation, or personal requests, regarding some aspect of his work in the church. In reality, such repeated attention is not always complimentay, but facetious flattery that the member practices to deceive this elder for reasons of having favors granted to him. Naturally, personality compliments will enable some members to approach one particular elder when a difference in other personality characteristics will not make it easy to talk with one of the other elders. However, differences in personality agreements is not the implication for this discussion, but rather the unhealthy, abnormal practice of elders being courted and paying court for reasons of pressure from party groups within the Lord's church. For illustration, there are preachers who have been known to indulge in the practice of political lobbying by persistently singling one elder out from the group, with private tete-a-tetes, in an attempt to have their own way, always. This error can be avoided, or overcome, by decisions being made in a majority vote of the elders, and never swayed by the dissenting voice of one man. If an individual member approaches one elder with an idea, request, or suggestion, this is normal human action and no abnormal reaction will be committed by either person when the elder takes the Christian's proposal before the eldership for decisive action.

When the membership of a congregation use such appellations as "the upper crust" and "the chosen few", in referring to their elders, there is indication of a wrong relationship existing between the two groups. Elders must always be mindful of the important difference allowed in choosing their personal friends,   for pleasantry in private society, and cliques within the congregation's membership which would interrupt the harmonious relationship of the Lord's people.

ELDERS AS PREACHERS

Elders must be "apt to teach", prepared in their knowledge of the Lord's Word to instruct other persons, to meet their scriptural obligation. However, for an elder of a designated congregation to be engaged in the full time pursuit of preaching in other locations is not advisable. If an elder decides to devote his talent to preaching the gospel, his decision is commendable, but impractical if he attempts to serve in both capacities, as an elder for one congregation and preacher for another. When an elder is away from the services of a church, nearly every week, preaching in other locations, his resignation from the eldership would be in the best interest of the congregation.

There are a few churches whose elders are almost all preachers, engaged in preaching for various congregations more Sundays than they are at home. This arrangement of their time divides their interest and leaves the church they serve as elders without shepherds most of the time. The work of either preacher or elder requires a man's full time devotion in preparation, and participation. When a two-level activity is attempted, the necessities involved in the dual responsibility renders one work being half-done. This is not to infer that an elder could not and should not contribute his talent for preaching occasionally from the pulpit of another congregation, but rather that he should not become a full time evangelist, participating in weekly engagements for other locations away from the eldership where he serves. The task of serving as an elder, held least in repute among men, has its necessary place of equal importance in God's plan for His work, as does the one that men regard highly. Those elders, whose work it is to "stay by the stuff" are deserving of as much credit and glory as the men who go forth to win the battle by preaching. All work needing to be done in the Lord's church deserves to be done well, without division of time and personal interest, with the realization that each Christian's work contributes to the growth of the church, and the spreading of the gospel of Christ. "Whatsoever thy hand findeth to do, do it with thy might." —Ecclesiastes 9:10.

CHAPTER V

ELDER-BROTHERHOOD RELATIONS

God's plan for the New Testament Church necessitates congregational independence, even though each organization is a stereotype of the apostolic churches of Christ. By the very economy of human nature, we are forced to realize that only infinite wisdom could have foreseen and prepared, with astute husbandry, this form of autonomous independency for each congregation. There is the existing fraternal society in Christianity of having a mutual interest in preaching the gospel, development of Christ's principles within humanity, and desire for growth in the Lord's churches that is the tie which binds the heart of the brotherhood. This common unity and peaceful co-existance with all other congregations we are commanded to maintain, if possible. The chief feelings and expectations regarding our fraternity for oneness, with scriptural approval of this brotherhood, is the subject matter for analytical consideration presented in this chapter.

CO-OPERATING WITH OTHER CONGREGATIONS

Congregations in various locations can co-operate and reciprocate in doing good works for the Lord without losing their autonomy, or without creating a separate body for governing a specific program undertaken in such joint action. There is power in a co-operative operation for realizing aims, plans, and purposes, but only power in the collective action and not invested in a hierarchical pontificate, composed of one group of men dictating to another group. Each eldership is commanded to oversee the work of one congregation, with no scriptural power for usurping authority over the elders and members of another church. While each group of elders may be of assistance to another, by assimilating ideas and combining forces to strengthen some particular endeavor undertaken together, each group should respect the practical adjustment of opinions, op-

posed views, or procedures for accomplishing their individual congregational work. One eldership should not be requested nor expected to compromise and sacrifice the fundamental principles of
God's policy for independent government in an attempt at adjustment, or settlement of differences. One eldership should not be expected to surrender to another group of elders under the pressured
demand for indulging the particular interest of the second group;
to do so, even for the sake of peace in the brotherhood, demands more
of elders than they can give in righteousness. In fact, the elders
involved in pressuring another group into submission to their wilfull plan are entirely out of harmony with God's plan for their operation.

Each congregation is under liability by the Law of Christ to do
its own work and when plans for a special effort require the
power of joint assistance, it is not unscriptural to seek co-operation
from another church in the brotherhood. However, it is an error of
attitude for the elders requesting co-operative association to exercise self-righteous pressure tactics when their solicitation is denied,
or refused. No endeavor is worthy, or can achieve acceptable conclusions, if its promoters create factious pressures upon another
group of Christians, by uncharitable criticism. The co-operation of
one congregation with another, one eldership co-ordinating plans
for some work with another eldership, must be a voluntary decision,
free from all coercion. If the elders approached decide against collaboration with the proposed program, because they believe that to
do so is in the best interest of their individual work, their decision
should be respected. Their refusal does not indicate that they are
wrong, nor that their handiwork should be pronounced as being insufficient. Neither is it necessary for an eldership to "line up" with
another eldership to be sound in doctrine, principles, or practice of
serving the Lord! Even if ninety-nine percent of all other congregations in the brotherhood are co-operating in a given program, the
one percent abstaining from supporting the project is not unscriptural. God did not accord the privilege of controlling the work of a

church to the ninety-nine, but only to one plurality of elders who solely make the decisions for acceptance, or rejection, of a program for the work within one congregation.

When an eldership is pressured into adopting some program, or swayed in its decision because of the desire to climb on a "band wagon" for prestige of human opinions when the project would interrupt their planned and worthy work, they lack strength of conviction. When elders are guilty of coercing another group of elders to join with their plans, whether they indulge in the popular practice of distributing written literature, or verbal denunciation for malicious slander, they demonstrate disinclination for obedience to the Lord by exercising zeal without knowledge. Perhaps, nothing has been more spurious and injurious to the cause of Christ, bringing more disparagement to those who strive to serve Him, than noisy and unreasoned zeal. Men who would create havoc, by practicing such attempts to persuade another group of elders to join with their plans, are not filled with virtuous fervor, but are sources of irritation to those whom they would win. They become meddlers in other elder's affairs, standing condemned in the Holy scriptures.

Co-operation among congregations in the brotherhood is capable of attaining perfection in achievement for worthy work, when this system of working together is in absolute harmony with God's revelation to man. The Lord did not give one group of elders jurisdiction over another body of elders; thus, there is no "brotherhood of elders" in the churches of Christ. The elders of each church are responsible for the work of the congregation, and their authority ends with the church over which they serve. All Christians may enjoy sweet peace, pleasant and agreeable experience in their endeavor of co-operation within the brotherhood, when elders recognize the importance of respecting privacy for one another's group decision. Each eldership must operate independently in reaching its conclusions for the church it oversees, firm in the knowledge that their leadership must answer to the Lord only, in submissive obedience.

LEARNING FROM OTHERS

Wise men learn by association with others while men of little understanding learn from their own limited experience, and the most ignorant learn only by necessity. Unfortunately, some elders are learners from the strict confines of the church in which they serve. This need not be the case for their limited learning with the numerous opportunities that elders now have for attending lecture-ships, which are planned and conducted throughout the brotherhood. The fact that these programs, designed for the express purpose of learning, are attended almost exclusively by preachers is depressing-ly pitiful. Elders need to take advantage of learning, by partici-pating in these lectureships, even if they need to arrange for time to be away from their secular business pursuits. A better and more prof-itable vacation time could not be spent than in attendance at some higher school for learning, such as a college lectureship, or other form of Christian workshop.

When elders seek to understand more improved ways for better effeciency in doing the Lord's work, they will redeem this time spent a hundred fold. Digestion of learning from joint thinking, listening, watching, gleaned from visiting with other leaders will increase the power of an eldership immeasurably. The recent experience of elders going to look at other church buildings in order to get a bet-ter perspective for the construction of their own edifice can be of as much value when moved into the other fields of their operation. El-ders do well to counsel with other leaders, combining ideas for a better clarification of methods and for more effeciency in expediting their individual programs.

The most profound illustration for stressing the importance of elders investigating a proven, workable system for doing the Lord's work is found in a budget program established by one group of el-ders being used repeatedly as a pattern by others. When this elder-ship decided to formulate a plan by which their financial program could be arranged in a more business like manner, they setup a proposed budget, requested the membership to support their estimated cost of operation by their individual purposeful contributions. These elders based their action on the example of the Corinthian church, setting their budgetary program into operation. There was unfounded, biased criticism from some quarters, but as the years have passed, proving the wisdom of their plan, this workable system has become a pattern to be used by other elders who have investigated their effective method. Vitality for strength, in achieving greater work in other areas of a church program, can be applied from this one illustration when elders realize the importance of learning from others.

SUPPORTING A PREACHER IN ANOTHER FIELD

Many congregations have grown strong enough in their individual programs to financially support the endeavor of a preacher in another location, in addition to their home base of operation. In this activity there can be great joy, reaping large harvests, when there is a respectful understanding of the positions for individual responsibility, by the overseeing elders and the preacher being supported in this type work. Without proper evaluation of the technique of such an operation, a man being supported in a work by a church for which he does not directly serve, some trifling misunderstandings can creep into the setup that can have far-reaching and harmful consequences for both parties.

When a man is wholly supported by one congregation, whether having been sent or having solicited his support, he is accountable to God for right and righteous usage of the money he receives. He is responsible for the trust placed in him by this church, and he is under the oversight of the elders who make his work possible. While he is isolated in carrying out his work, being perhaps far away from his base of operation, he is obligated to furnish the overseeing eldership a periodical report that is informative and comprehensive in relating the details of his accomplishments. This preacher is obligated to furnish the overseeing eldership a periodical report that is informative and comprehensive in relating the details of his accomplishments. This preacher is obliged to accord the supporting eldership the same degree of consideration, respect, and honor, as the man who preaches within their building each week. He is to be governed by their authority in meeting their requirements for his work, conforming to their major decisions, as if he served within the congregation overseen by them daily. If he plans to move his location of work, he should advise these elders of his plans in advance of the departure date, and reach an agreement with them about this matter. The behavior of a preacher being unwilling to serve under the guidance of elders is contrary to the Lord's plan for his work, and displays his personal abandonment to embalance, with both the work and himself being unworthy of financial support.

Elders are under the self-sameness for scriptural balance in their relationship with a preacher being supported in another field, as in their relation with the local preacher. They have the same obligation for consideration in supporting him with human sympathy, as in their financial support. They must be kind, patient, understanding, and ready always to encourage him in his work. Should they decide to discontinue their support of his work for any reason, the same consideration for allowing the man ample time to re-locate must be accorded him, as if he were serving their local work. They are obligated to advise this preacher in advance of any change in their support which they might deem necessary, or wise. If the man is serving in another country, he should be given time and financial aid for returning to the continental bounderies of his own country, with the consideration for securing other supported work. Sending a preacher to a foreign country necessitates a longer range plan than for one sent to some stateside location in the assurance of continued support for him and for his work. An eldership should "count the cost" before taking the responsibility for sending a preacher into a foreign mission field, since there are more financial involvements in this type program.

SUPPORTING A PREACHER IN CO-OPERATIVE EFFORT

When more than one congregation co-operates in a combined financial effort for supporting the work of a preacher in another field, this man should be under the oversight and answerable to the eldership responsible for initiating the program. There is no more wisdom nor scriptural justification for a mission preacher to operate in a "free lance", unsupervised fashion than for a local preacher to serve under the same lack of elder oversight. The examples of New Testament preachers serving under the direction of an eldership, while being supported in their work by the contributions of several congregations, is concise. This rule, or God's law, for action of conduct in sending forth mission preachers is the same accepted method of behavior today, as during the days of the apostolic church, and should be violated for no reason whatsoever.

There need be no argument concerning which eldership should oversee the man who is doing a mission work and who is receiving co-ordinated support from more than one congregation. There need be no anxiety, concern, or fear that too much power and honor will be accorded the elders directing this operation of work. The futility of such thinking can be assuaged by righteous reasoning, as well as a common sense approach to the subject, revealing that such an arrangement gives the supervising eldership no more power than it would have if it supported this man alone. Since scriptural direction necessitates the work of a preacher being done under the oversight of one eldership, it is both unscriptural and unreasonable to assume that he should be overseen by a half-dozen groups of elders, located throughout various parts of the country. Naturally, the eldership who initiated and sponsored the solicited co-operation of the other elders would be better qualified to fully understand the mission because they would have investigated every intricate detail of the proposed program. There can be no deleterious effect upon the efficiency, or ultimate achievement, for the congregations combining forces in this joint effort of supporting a particular work, with the engaged preacher serving under the oversight of the one eldership. In fact, any other arrangement would be to disregard God's principle of order, established for directing any program of church operation by the Lord Himself. The elders who are contributing factors in such a combined operation do not relinquish any authority of their individual rights, but can enjoy the peace of confidence found in a right relationship with God and their fellow-elders. Their assurance can be absolute in the knowledge that a capable eldership is looking after their joint effort of collaborated work in sending a man to preach the gospel of Christ to some corner of the world where they cannot personally go, or afford to support independently this mission program.

It is an important factor to the harmony and success of this type of co-operative function that each group of contributing elders be furnished with a regular, detailed, report; this will afford distributive information concerning the segment, progress, and achievement of their supported work. It is inconsequential as to who furnishes this report to the various elderships, whether it is sent out by the man in the mission location, or by the eldership under whom he serves dispatching copies of the reports sent directly to them. If the elders responsible for this program of co-operative effort fail to oversee the work properly, or if the mission preacher fails to accomplish the work for which he was sent in a satisfactory manner, the same power sending the joint contributions can withdraw their individual support. When elders decide to withdraw support from a co-operative endeavor, however, they should give considerate notification to the supervising eldership of their intention, properly stating their reason for the withdrawal. As in all other relations between human beings, their declaration for withdrawing support may be dependent upon some human misunderstanding that could be clarified and not interrupt the work of preaching the gospel. When all work of the Lord is done "decently and in order" it is pleasing to God.

PLANNING OTHER CONGREGATIONS

There are two conditions to petition the genuine need for a thriving congregation considering, planning, building, and supporting a newly located church. The first is when a community is not being served by an existing congregation. The second reason is when a church building has outgrown its local inhabitants, requiring duplication of Sunday services for membership accommodation. Either one of these substantial evidences for the need of another congregation in a nearby vicinity is very often created by the growth of population in a community, or because of the expansion of their city limits by increased subdivisions.

When there exists the validity for a congregation to establish another one, the economy of a given situation will determine the amount of financial and supervisory support which will be needed by the new group, as well as for the duration of time this aid will be required. There are instances when a new congregation is formed that assistance from the older church is not needed and only the blessing and prayers of the brethren which gave them birth is requested. There are cases when a congregation erects the newly located building and affords partial financial aid, for the new work, until the infant group is able to be self-supporting. The danger involved in a congregation receiving partial financial support from another is that too much, for too long, can be done for the new group. The stronger church can become a "crutch" rather than an aid to the smaller church, which would offer no challenge for their energies and no satisfaction for their own achievements. Therefore, this danger necessitates that caution and wisdom be exercised by the assisting congregation.

The desirability, from the viewpoint of fewer human difficulties being incurred, of a new congregation not being begun until all aspects of the internal qualifications make it self-sustaining is evident. However, there are instances when the need for organizing a new group is required and the infant congregation begun, which entails supervision by the elders instigating its origin. Until men qualified to serve as elders are known and appointed for the new group, it would be a shepherdless flock without the oversight of the eldership of the older church. In New Testament history there is the record of one church in one city, but this does not infer that the needs of a city population, and distance of city bounderies in present day circumstances coincide with the same needs of Biblical history cities. The criteria of New Testament record does not infer that it is wrong to have more than one congregation in a modern day city, when the populace of a community warrants more than one church. This operation is simply substantiated by common sense reasoning when more than one congregation is established in order to accommodate the needs of the people. Therefore, if common sense reasoning can establish them, common sense thinking can keep them operating in harmony with the scriptural injunction that the government of a church is to be overseen by an eldership.

To such an ambiguous question,"Who ever heard of one group of elders, appointed for the oversight in one church, serving over another group?," the self-same lack of reasoning would ask, "Who ever heard of one New Testament congregation sponsoring the building of another in the same city limits?" A justifiable answer to both questions is found in the realm of righteous reasoning and common sense balance in thinking, which is the reliability of mental capacity given by God to man's nature, elevating him above the level of animals. When the membership met together in their old location, they met in different rooms to study the Bible for one hour and were under the oversight of one eldership. When their growth exceeded their building capacity for seating the entire membership during one hour of worship service, two separate times for worship was regulated. Yet, for the duration of their double services, separating the body of these Christian people, the overall program continued to be directed by one eldership. The difference between the needs of an infant congregation, which grew out of the over crowded situation of the older church, is a number of blocks from one building location to the other. For just so long as the infant group needs supervision from the eldership which gave birth to them, is the duration of time that these elders should continue to serve over their work. Of course, just as soon as the newly formed group has qualified men, they should be appointed as elders, then the former eldership would no longer have a scriptural reason to oversee their work. Each congregation must have its independent eldership to be in harmony with the Lord's Will, which necessitates an appointment of this body of men as soon as equitable in all infant churches. However, until such appointments are possible, it is reasonable that the requirements of God's plan be met by the new congregation receiving supervision from the eldership of the older church.

A justifiable reason for the inception of a new congregation is best illustrated by the growth of a certain church. Their membership had grown to the proportion that two morning worship services were required, filling their building to capacity for both appointed hours. Their structure was uncomfortably crowded for the evening worship hour. Years before the eldership of this group had used wisdom and vision in purchasing a building site in one of the growing sections of this city, in their long range planning for establishing another congregation some day. The time had arrived when their vision was rewarded. The growth of the congregation made it advisable to support the birth of a new church. The expansion program was launched, and the building near completion when those who lived nearer the location of this new building expressed their desire to work and worship there. Among this group of members were several men who were qualified to comprise an eldership; they were selected and appointed by those going to the new work location. Therefore, this was an ideal arrangement, when the concepted dreams for a new congregation became a living reality, the new edifice readied for inhabitance, all things were readied for a self-contained church with a fully organized and growing work begun. A sufficient debt balance was left unpaid on the new building to inspire the membership towards growth and development; which demand of effort is spiritually healthy. The success of this new congregation was dependent upon order and decent organization of planning from its inception. The success of its habitation in growth and development was based upon harmony, unison, and Christian love, founded upon a sincere desire for good work attainment.

New congregations should not be given life for reasons that lack scriptural justification for their coming into being, or for their existance. To mention a few of the unholy reasons for the establishment of some congregations are human disagreements among a body of Christians; self-judgment and disapproval of a preacher or of the elders; desire for self-exhalation in some men desiring an appointment to the church leadership, to which position they might aspire to attain by forming a new congregation; an over estimation of the importance for having a plurality of congregations in a city, even though the criteria of population and city limits belie such need. Any one of these compelling forces making up the element of human conflict would not be resolved by Christians moving to a new location, nor substantiate the excuse for dividing a church membership in building a new one. People can never find resolvable peace for their souls, nor forgiveness for their human errors, in a new church building. If the heart is right, brethren can dwell together in harmonious respect under all circumstances of personality differences, settling all grievances having to do with a differing of human opinions.

Too many times there are instances when a strong congregation has been divided in number, hindered in growth, stunted in development, by branching out to form a new group before there was a genuine need for this action. There is strength in numbers, both physically as well as financially, and there can be unity combined with strength in a numerically large church. It is factual knowledge that most of the mission preaching and benevolent work being done in the brotherhood of churches is attained by congregations of larger size then by smaller ones; not because God places a premium on bigness, but because numerically larger groups are financially more able to reach farther out, beyond their local programs, and engage in more extensive works. It is also the common practice for the larger and stronger congregations to be thought about and contacted first whenever assistance is needed for some large scale program of work in the brotherhood. Therefore, the misconception, expressed by many of the brethren, that a Christian can find more individual work to do in a smaller church belies the actual sources for co-operation sought, and accomplishments wrought.

RECOGNIZING AND RESPECTING DECISIONS

The Bible emphatically gives instructions for the acceptable reasons for Christians withdrawing fellowship from persons who are proven guilty of malpractice in living by the precepts and principles of Christ, in such a manner as to bring injurious reflection upon the Lord's church. However, the Biblical teachings are no less specific for instructing the associate-Christians of a fallen, or straying, brother in their responsibility for human efforts to restore such a member. When the scripture has been fulfilled, all has been done that is possible in righteous effort to restore an errant brother, he rejects all admonition and refuses to be obedient to God's law, it becomes the unpleasant duty of the elders to make an announcement of withdrawal to the congregation over which they serve. This action constitutes what is known as "withdrawing fellowship" and such a plight is sad work for the elders, saddens the church membership, places the guilty soul in jeopardy of God's judgment, but should be gravely respected by all churches in the brotherhood.

When there is such a serious case of a Christian's misconduct, resulting in the necessity of an eldership announcing withdrawal from one, all the information of facts with documented proof is imperative for escaping the possibility of mistake, which would involve human judgment. One eldership should not expect the elders of another location to act upon their withdrawal announcement without being ready, willing, and able to produce positive proof to support their solemn recommendation. If the person from whom fellowship has been withdrawn moves his attendance to another congregation, persisting in the practice of sinful, disobedient living, he should not be received in full fellowship by a church in another location. Otherwise, the action taken against him can produce no good fruit, either from the errant brother or the Lord's church. The action of withdrawing fellowship is the ultimate in human effort for bringing a person to repentance and into submission to Christ. This can never be achieved by the meritorious and painful action of one group of elders if another group welcome this rebellious soul, with a banner of approval, by accepting an unvirtuous, flagrant life of sin. It is the rightful duty for the elders of a church, when a rebuked person is seeking fellowship, to investigate the previously made charges of another eldership because no group of men is infallible. The decisions of one eldership is not the final judgment, only the Lord is the Chief Shepherd.

It is not at all uncommonly human for individuals to be too severe in the judgments they mete out to another, consequently even elders may err in passing judgment upon another. This is a territory so filled with the possibility of human error that makes the act of withdrawing fellowship extremely dangerous. This Biblical justification for such action can only be based upon positive proof of immoral, flagitious, iniquitous, or riotious practice of living for a professed Christian, in being such flagrant shamefulness as to bring reproach upon the Lord's church and upon His people. There have been rare cases when men have been denounced and dis-fellowshipped without scriptural justification and proof. Therefore, the brethren withdrawing from another because of a clash in personality differences, variance in human opinions and decisions that involves no wrongful action on the accused's part, stand in dire jeopardy of God's judgment for their malicious accusations. It is unholy for Christians to use the idea of fellowship as a whiplash against another soul in pressure group ideas of human concepts. In view of the few cases of such a miscarriage of justice and because elders must deal equitably with all persons, each individual case of a previous withdrawal of fellowship should be investigated on its own merit.

There have been some isolated cases of brethren refusing fellowship to another on the basis of a difference in human conception for certain practices, or methods, for doing the Lord's work; recognized as being expedient in one particular location, but branded as "Error" by groups in another locale. For illustration, there is considerable variance in human opinion regarding the disputed subject of having a designated room within the walls of a church building for the purpose of fellowship gatherings. God gave no instruction concerning this matter, whether to have or not to have such rooms, but left the method to man's discretion for carrying out His expressed commandment that Christians should be hospitable. The Lord directs His people to have spiritual communion, mutual interest in association one with the other, with many examples of Christians engaging in social fellowship during apostolic times. However, as in other areas for promoting the work and growth of the church, the practice for utilizing whatever commodious conveniences are practical, God leaves entirely up to the quality of human reasoning. While there are realms in which man is obliged to acknowledge that human reason cannot, dare not, penetrate insofar as compliance with the Lord's expressed commandments, reliance upon human reason is the glory of man's mentality that can be a glorious asset in strengthening the work which God wants done, in matters employing realism. When brethren refuse to fellowship with another simply because he believes in the commodity of practical reasoning, being combined with Divine Instruction, for doing the Lord's work, such refusal is human and without Biblical foundation. Those brethren who wrest the scriptures, in a frustrating search for common sense "know how", make few constructive decisions and very often wrong one of their brothers. Elders should diligently search and abide by the Holy Word when making a decision, so fearfully close to the realm of human judgment, before refusing to fellowship a Christian brother, or sister.

The scriptural implication in refusing a Christian fellowship is the restriction barring him from public service participation, such as teaching a Bible class, serving at the Lord's Table, and leading in prayers of the assembly. Also, Christian fraternization, such as public social acceptance, is to be denied an errant brother until he would repent his manner of living. There is no instruction from the Lord, however, refusing a wayward brother in privilege of worshipping in an assembly of the church, or of denying him the right to eat the Lord's Supper. Each soul is subject unto God, with the prayerful hope of all Christians for deliverance from a chosen life of sin by the repentance of each person, denying attendance to a disobedient brother goes beyond the realm of Divine Word and makes no more common sense than denying attendance to an unbeliever! The Lord rejoices over the return to the fold of one of His lost lambs. As long as a soul is on this side of heaven is the duration for prayerful hope of his repentance by his Christian brethren.

There is advisability for avoiding much difficulty by teaching Christian people the wisdom in their requesting a letter of recognition when they leave one congregation and move to another location. This is a practice of some churches, while others write a letter back to the previous eldership, which a person declares to have left, requesting information concerning the one placing membership. In most cases the inquiry is honored with an immediate reply, but occasionally no answer is received by the inquiring eldership. The practice of receiving declared members of the church in full fellowship, of belief and trust, has in some instances proven detrimental to the well-being of a congregation. In this age of various forms of subversive activities and error in human intentions, elders would exercise scriptural wisdom by following New Testament example in teaching their people to request a letter of introduction. Such a letter would serve as both recognition and recommendation when Christians change membership from one church location to another. This intelligent procedure would serve the elders, as well as the individual brother. A Bible teacher could be recognized immediately

C.3087

by the former elder's recommendation of accomplished work, whereas without this knowledge the elders in the new location would need time to learn of this qualification. A congregation could be in need of leadership and a letter of introduction could serve to recommend a man who had such ability. In addition to the sound reasons for the advantage to an eldership being the recipient of this type of letter, the individual who bears a letter of introduction can be encouraged to carry on his desired work, in a new church home, without waste of energy and time.

CONFIDENCE IN THE BROTHERHOOD

Confidence expressed in one another, among churches within the brotherhood, is basic to the element of spreading the gospel of Christ throughout the world. Without belief and reliance upon the integrity of other congregations, the entire structure of Christianity is weakened. Confidence is our strengthening, human agent for standing united in Christian works of progress, and in presenting a strong, impregnable armour against the hoard of religious dividers. Division in the brotherhood is capable of wrecking havoc among churches, despair within Christians, both condemned by God. Disrespectful lack of confidence is not evidenced because of differences in doctrine, but most often because of ignorance among brethren. However, being innocent of conscious wrongdoing, yet guilty of creating division deserves condemnation; for, ignorance does not justify nor remove the Lord's judgment. An illustration of innocent ignorance is the incident related in the experience of a preacher's encounter with several other ministers, which occurred during their luncheon together. This man was a visiting evangelist, engaged in a meeting away from his large home congregation. Sometime in the course of his pleasant conversation with these local preachers, he was asked the question, "Do you preach such doctrinal sermons in your home church, as you are preaching in the services of this gospel meeting?" The evangelist replied with an affirmative answer and added, "As a matter of fact, these particular sermons I composed and preached to my home congregation." Following a few minutes of silence, the visiting man inquired, "Why did you ask this question?" The inquisitor's response was an honest, straightforward admission of the innocent ignorance directing his attitude, "I have always heard that a man could not preach for a large church membership and remain positive in delivering doctrinal sermons." There are many sincere people so misinformed in the brotherhood. They are often guilty of criticizing numerically large congregations, as a product of innocent ignorance, mentally doubting the doctrinal soundness of these groups. Unfortunately, this misconceived and erronous thinking has spread, like bad news, throughout certain areas of churches in the brotherhood.

An equal responsibility is shared by those persons who believe an untruth, by listening, with those individuals who believe an erronous thought and express their ideas, by speaking. The speaker cannot propagate a story, true or false, unless there is a hearer. Very often, the lack of confidence that churches in one sector of the country have in churches in another section of our nation has come about entirely on the basis of hearsay. These disheartening rumors are usually given birth by unlearned, frustrated human beings; frequently, one who sustained some feeling of personal injury, through a misunderstanding, has moved away harboring the emotional grudge of not getting a "square deal" by someone else. The work and attitude of one person should never be the basis for jumping to a conclusion, or for forming an opinion about another congregation. In our day, of fast communications, a person can hear almost anything in the way of hearsay information about another group of of Christians, if a hearer for long! Most often, sincere investigation will prove all critical reports to be false and without factual foundation.

For illustration of some hearsay stories, which are popular tidbits of conversation that brethren parrot about various churches, are these: "Why, I wouldn't go back to that church for love nor money!

The only subject their preacher knows and lectures on is money; they're either financially hard-up, or he's money crazy!" When this source of gossip is learned, it is to learn that once, or twice, this person attended with six months having lapsed between visits and the sermon needfully preached was on Christian responsibility for giving; these lesson texts concided with the two occasions of this member's attendance. Another misguiding remark is, "Why, I wouldn't go back to that church if I never attended another service; that is the coldest church I've ever visited and I went several times!" Factually, that person most likely sat on the backward pews and left the building on the breath of the final amen, as though shot from a gun. One of the local members would have needed track shoes, necessary for running a fifty yard sprint, to catch and welcome this visitor. Sometimes, a peeved, displaced, ex-member of a certain congregation will furnish this choice morsel of gossip, "It is as hard to break-in and belong to the clique of that church as to get into the White House! Everything is done by one select group and if you don't belong to that set, you're nothing!" The truth would reveal that for the duration of whatever the months, or years, this member was a part of that church, he was a nonentity, insomuch as offering to be of personal service, whatsoever. He envied the work and attainments of others, but put forth no individual effort of contributing to the program. There is the case of a mother who broadcast the report from her teenage child's report about a class, wherein the method of debate was being used on the occasion of her visit, "My daughter could never go back to that church; she visited in their Sunday evening class and was a living witness in hearing the division which existed there on the subject of dancing." One visit of one young girl instigated the rumor of unsound doctrinal teachings within the classes of a congregation. "I'm moving to "Timbuckto" and would like to place membership with the Treeshoe congregation, but it's run by Bro. Coiza, you know! He has been there a hundred years, ramrods that church, and I couldn't worship with an unscriptural group." The dementia provoking this caustic statement stems from the popular illusion that when a minister remains longer than five years in a congregation, he automatically becomes a dictator and the eldership no more than a figurehead to serve his whims. The other scripturally unfounded heresays are too numerous to mention. However, the value of all such rumors is worthless and elders must ever be cautiously on their guard against believing this type of information. As the shepherds of the Lord's household, if such error should creep into their thinking it can spill over and become the attitude of churches toward other congregations throughout the brotherhood. Harmony has been replaced by discord, with no more solid foundation than hearsay has evolved into malicious gossip, retarding growth of the Lord's church through lack of co-operation in the brotherhood.

Inhabitants of the churches of Christ are human beings and as such will always be subject to committing some form of error. There are instances when an entire congregation will become erroneous in practice, which should create sorrow and not public condemnation among other churches. In a world filled to over-flowing with error of one kind or another, truth and love one for the other can be the only acceptable weapons for combatting error within the brotherhood. It would seem that there are some few preachers who spend more time searching out what they believe to be errors among brethren, spending more hours in broadcasting their findings, than they spend in searching the Holy scripture for preaching better gospel sermons! God gives explicit instruction for the method to be applied in assisting an errant brother. There is no Biblical Word, nor example, for the practice of writing "an open letter to the brotherhood," denouncing the error of another person or group of people. The Lord condemns public denunciation of brother against brother, either by means of a tree-top, radio, television, or challenge to an open discussion; with pre-advertizement for public invitation. Nehemiah said, when invited by Sanballat and Geshem to meet in one of the villages in the plain of Ono for a discussion, "I am doing a good work: why should the work cease, whilst I leave it, and come down to you?"

A church, cannot do its best work while its members are engaged in being busybodies. Love, longsuffering, meekness, gentleness, and goodness are four of the ninefold fruits of the Spirit that should prevail in the attitude of brethren. Confidence one in the other, among individual Christians, elderships, and churches, will produce usefulness to God and the oneness of purpose necessary for converting the world. There is no value in a sound doctrine unless the people are made sound by the New Testament knowledge.

CHAPTER VI

YOU AND YOUR ELDERS

The primary aim of this book is to stimulate and strengthen the leadership of the Lord's church, by portraying some of the difficulties created by human nature that hinder their relationship. While elders are responsible for planning, directing, and overseeing all programming of a congregation's work, each Christian has a share in the accountability for its success. Thus, the purport of this written endeavor would not be complete without the inclusion of this chapter. Individual members of the Lord's church owe an allegiance to their elders, second only to the Lord. "Obey them that have the rule over you, and submit yourselves: for they watch for your souls, as they that must give account, that they may do it with joy, and not with grief: for that is unprofitable for you." This is the Divine command, recorded in the Hebrew letter, and while this chapter will broach the topic from the common sense viewpoint, it will be in harmonious correlation with the Law of Christ.

UNDERSTAND YOUR ELDERS

Elders are men of strong faith, thoughtful wisdom, and obedient minds to God; but no less human in nature than any other Christian. They have the same emotional capacities for disappointment, discouragement, and grief as they have for satisfaction, optimism, and joy. Elders are human beings who laugh when happy, cry when sad. While God wrote the rule for their office appointments, He did not create them with built-in, super-human qualities. These men are the appointed shepherds of the Lord's flock, but they have the self-same conquest of self-mastery, as we all strive to conquer. All men's moods may vary, in the day-to-day physiological conditions of life, from gaiety to melancholy, and elders like other Christians fight this battle of human disposition. We need love, sympathy, and human compassion in combination with grateful appreciation for our elders, to be competently able to enter into a relationship of mutual feeling with these men.

Double-duty is the work of an elder, encompassed in his secular business pursuit and his attendance to the business of the Lord's house. Whatever the entailments of his earthly enterprise, by which he earns bread and butter, he spends countless, unremunerated monetary, hours in his church labor. This man faces the same competition in his burdens of commercial work as any other man, with the usual work-day hours required of him. In addition to this business is the weighty hours requiring his time in the business of the church. It is significant, therefore, that with the precious commodity of time being equal for all men, the toiled hours of an elder's labor often continues while his Christian companions sleep. These hours of planning, praying, and working for happy growth of a congregation are wearisome ones, but perfect the masterpieces for upbuilding the Lord's flock and achieving perfected work for a church. This self-denial is evident of the honor, submission, and gratefulness that should be every member's attitude toward an elder. The plans made for the development of a congregation, by our elders, are to help relieve the tedium of much wasted talent and energy of each one of us. Their constant watchfulness is the valve to our spiritual safety, in maintaining vigilance over our weaknesses and our needs. This ever-present care could not be for vain-glory, from a selfish heart, but that portion of an elder's life that is poured out in self-sacrifice and unselfish service founded upon love for God first; others second, self last.

OUR BEST FRIENDS ARE ELDERS

Elders desire to be friends to each one of the membership over which they serve, since part of their responsibility is satisfied in the meaning of the word "friend." Their friendship inclines them to be genuinely interested in our welfare and wellbeing. Elders are honest men who accept the obligation to oversee, not fleece, the flock; they will share our experiences whether sad or glad, rich or poor.

These men participate in the sharing of all work which they plan, with no intention of demanding the impossible from anyone. Their friendship does not exist on self-interest, but on unselfish love, with sincere concern for our physical and spiritual wellbeing. When we do not look to them as our friends, our own selfish unfaithfulness has broken the bond of their proffered love for us. Their friendship is offered to us in overt acts of kindness, and in their practice of living as our examples to follow into eternal life with God.

The affection of their friendliness should produce an atmosphere between us favorable for inviting us to freely discuss our problems with them. They are not meddlers into our affairs, but friends desirous of helping to lighten our burdens, whatever they may be in nature. Elders are not gossipers and Christians should develop more confidence for talking uninhibitedly with them, their concern is in helping to alleviate our sorrows. When an individual member feels that there is a "wall" between himself and the elders, he has been the contractor for this mental barrier. Naturally, since all Christians are human beings with varying personalities, there will always be one elder with whom we will feel a closer tie, deeper bond of understanding, and a greater degree of free expression. In other words, the tendrils of man's spirit in individuality will be attracted to the elder most akin to his own personality. If, however, not one of the men making up the body of our elders is felt to be a friend, the fault is our own without doubt. This is an indictment against our disallowance of an elder's friendship and we should tear down that wall, accept their friendly help, and "know those who watch over our souls."

ELDERS DESERVE OUR SUPPORT

Obligatory is the Holy Command upon each Christian for wholehearted support and assistance to our elder's programming of work. These men spend exhaustive hours of tireless efforts for our benefit, as well as for growth of the church. They are willing to lead us along the pathway that we should follow in our work for the Lord.

Common sense knowledge dictates that our elders cannot lead unless we will be led; for, there is no strength of leadership, regardless of its qualifications, unless people are willing to follow. Each member has his own work obligation, measured according to his personal ability, and if left undone a hole is left gapping in the church program. Our elders fulfill their sacred trust by planning and leading the various aspect of our work; we must fulfill our duty to God by our willing and cheerful support of their program plans. Elders are not infallible and there are some few instances when the best intended plans are not successfully attained; but, each member's liability is whether or not this failure was dependent upon his insupport.

For clarification of the many ways that support and help can be given to our elders, which mutual relationship is necessary for completeness in their plans, are the ensuing methods. First, full attendance support to all services, insomuch as humanly possible is the acknowledgement of our debt owed to the elders arranging these occasions for glorifying God. They do not plan services for their personal glory. When an evangelistic meeting is planned, our wholehearted endeavor should be applied for personal attendance, as well as for inviting our neighbors to go with us to hear the gospel preached. In addition to our attendance support, we should extend our willingness to be hospitable with our homes, by entertaining the preacher and other visiting saints. Any other personal service that we can render to the successful accomplishment of their plan for evangelism, we should make available to our elders.

We should assist our elders by answering their call for all special services, such as Vacation Bible Schools, Training for Service Series, Teacher Training classes. We should not sit back, waiting to see whether or not someone else will do the required work, but volunteer our help immediately, with whatever individual ability we can contribute. There is no justification in our words of excuse, "I do not feel that I am able to serve." The benevolent work of visiting the aged shut-ins, hospitalized Christians, taking food to the needy, and talking with someone who is anxious to learn the way of salvation, is just to mention a few of the numerous channels of the elder's program, in which we can be of personal assistance. When we are unable to assist them with a particular work, we should make ourselves available for the next call.

Our thoughtfulness in offering any constructive suggestion that might aid our elders to facilitate their programming of work can be of invaluable help. Elders are always anxious to learn of any method that may better their work; realizing that some ideas for methods that were progressive in one location may not serve in their program. Our responsibility is to offer whatever suggestions we believe might prove beneficial, but not to become peeved and offended if our ideas are not considered to be acceptable ones for practice in our elder's work. While some suggestions might be valuless, others may prove of great value. Our most worthy asset is our attitude in all respects, disposition, as well as ability and wholehearted support. When we live in obedient harmony to the Lord, the program of our church, and with other people, our elders are relieved of much painful effort in their responsibility for shepherding the flock.

We contribute worthy assistance by listening to our own elders, not being led astray by some outside voice that is speaking in contradiction to them; such voices are without authority from God. There are always those among us, as self-appointed "watch dogs" and "sheeps in wolves clothing" who, by their meddling, will destroy the unity in every congregation where the members will listen. They do not hesitate to procure a church membership roster for the purpose of distributing their divisive literature among members of a serene Christian group. Instead of being "tossed to and fro by every wind of doctrine," we can talk frankly with our elders about anything that is prone to disturb the harmony within our congregation. We should refuse, with a steadfast purpose, to support anyone who would destroy the influence of our elders with our hearing. Never should we be guilty of being led into a meeting where a person is offering a plan that is in opposition to the advocated program of our elders.

Giving of our material blessings is commanded to be done by "Every man according as he purposeth in his heart," which when correlated with the elder's responsibility for financial budgetary of a church infers that we should afford them a knowledge of our purposing. Common sense thinking informs us that without forehanded information as to the amount which individual members purpose to give for supporting the Lord's work, our elders cannot adequately plan for the cost of this operation. After all, they are not endowed with clairvoyant power for seeing non-existant dollars! It is foolish and childish thinking when Christians "hide" from elders their purposed giving, because the One to whom they give sees all. Sick is the depravity of a soul attempting to hide the sin of covetousness behind such words as "It is nobody's business how much I give to my Lord!" Such lame excuses as, "The denominations do it that way!" do not conceal a miserly heart from God. When an adult Christian says, "I can't let the elders know what amount I will give because I don't know whether or not I will continue to earn as much as I am making now; our nation's economy looks bad, you know!" In this conversation there are three sins made manifest, lack of faith, anxiety, and miserliness. We reveal our ignorance of Divine Teaching, Biblical examples, and disrespect to our elders when we refuse them the knowledge of our financial purpose in giving. We are obligated to furnish this information to them willingly and cheerfully, with assurance that the amount represents a liberal portion of our income. If purposing our Lord's contribution is a shortcoming of our individual understanding, our elders need to know for the purpose of instructing us in righteousness. This is one personal way each member can help the elders in watching for our soul's salvation.

Confidence in our elders is expressed by our action of trusting in their ability and integrity to direct our contribution in all fruitful ventures. There are many worthwhile places that are needful of support, but it is not possible for one congregation to afford aid to every person who is seeking assistance. We cannot be in all places, at all times. It is one duty of our elders to decide the best places for sending the support of our congregation. There have been cases when a person felt it was his prerogative to choose the work which he would independently support. This is lack of sound reasoning, since the elders are obliged to plan all aspects of the church work and this portion comes under their jurisdiction, also. If one member usurped the privilege of sending his contribution wherever he chose, all members could act likewise, with lack of order prevailing in this work of a church program. The courage of an eldership is to be admired in its words toward a member, determined to operate in a "free lance" fashion of sending his financial contribution to places undesignated by them, in suggesting that he would be happier in the location supported by his money! The church in which we have membership, under whose eldership we serve, has prior claim on us. We can assist our shepherds, contribute to the growth of the Lord's church, and make our souls safer if we submit to these elders, with thanksgiving to God for them.

ELDERS DESERVE OUR RESPECT

From a preacher's point of view, my resentment is justified in loathing mistreatment of ministers by elders. The misbegotten concept that as a hired servant the preacher can be treated like a slave is abominable. Worse is my abhorrence for mistreatment of the elders, by preachers and other "so-called" Christians. Some people treat elders worse than infidels, or the worst enemy of the church. The labors of an elder are too frequently a thankless job, unappreciated properly by most Christians. These devout men need and deserve spoken words of encouragement, expressions of gratitude, from all of us. We show forth disrespect as well as uncharitable spirits, when we fail to acknowledge our appreciation to these worthy men, occasionally.

To profess devotion to God, while guilty of a critical attitude toward our elders, is to "mouth" our love for Him! No man is perfect, everyone has his faults, and elders are human beings. As a general rule, these men are doing the best they can, erring seldom as a collective group, and our criticism sinfully increases the burden of their yoke. If an elder should make an honest mistake and is in need of constructive criticism, we should respectfully speak to him in private; never be guilty of fault-finding publicly, nor criticize him to others. There have been some few places where one elder, sometimes more than one, was the topic for gossip and critical discussion among groups gathered for social events. Some groups have criticized elders so much, for so long, that the very mention of their names obligates the speaker to buy coffee for all who heard his slip of the tongue!

As a general rule, upon investigation, that the person habituated to criticizing an elder fits into one of several slots of emotional frustration, by some disappointment, such as personal failure in being appointed as a deacon, or as an elder; provoked because a personal preacher friend wasn't the selected, or invited, evangelist; rejection of some proposed idea, or suggestion; a person whose dissolute manner of action has been rebuked by an elder, at some time. Genuine Christianity does not allow such misconduct, and submission to our elders will inscribe respect at all times on the banner of the heart. We cannot be unkind to those appointed to do the Lord's work, without being unkind to the Lord. Our respect for God is epitomized in the proportionate degree shown our elders.

Preachers have been known to be culprits, stained with the guilt of habitually criticizing their elders; not constructive criticism, spoken within the security of individual privacy, but publicly. For illustration of the heart break that can be created within the Lord's church when a preacher is disrespectful toward elders we relate two factual, not hypothetical, cases that happened. A preacher moved into a congregation to begin working and among his first visitors were a few enemies of a certain elder. Because of malevolent, disrespectful comments, this preacher formed an opinion of ill-will toward the elder. The result was that he built-up a mental barrier, separating himself from this good man, which the elder was unable to tear down with all his friendly persuasion. This separation produced unprofitable fruit and the preacher finally moved away, never realizing that his failure was the product of his own making. He had been guilty of hearing and believing the criticism of unworthy persons about a genuinely devout elder.

Another incident of a preacher's mistreatment of elders is in the true case of a certain church hiring a minister who was a "wolf in sheep's clothing." He had assured the eldership of a newly formed congregation that his disposition toward certain benevolent works was in harmony with their program. When this group was financially able to support some of these works, their decision was in favor of co-operating with other congregations in supporting a certain home for orphaned children. From the onset of the preacher's work, he had been deceitfully gathering a following of the church membership around him, propagating his distorted viewpoints. When the elders' decision was made to the congregation for helping these homeless children, the membership was divided. This preacher became so vindictive in his attitude towards the elders that they decided to resign and leave their work there. Their wisdom in deciding to resign and abandon the congregation is questionable, only God is qualified to sit in judgment here. However, this preacher and the members guilty of malfeasant, disrespectful threatment of these elders cannot. be exonerated.

A faithful elder died, no doubt sooner than necessary, under the burden of grief from the pressure of injustice brought to bear upon him by members in a particular church. The disturbing factor was brought about by a preacher's infidelity for abiding by his working agreement with this eldership. He repeatedly broke his agreement as to the number of times he was to be away from the congregation, leaving his local work improperly attended creating dissatisfaction

but not dismissal. Finally, he planned to be away for a lengthy duration and in a dishonest gesture of attempted justification for his
action, he wrote a letter of resignation, as a threat to the elders if
they objected to his absence. The elders accepted his resignation,
much to his surprise! Then, his deceitful intention was shown by
his action in gathering a group of disgruntled followers, from the membership, around himself and proceeded on his malicious course against
one of the elders. This group brought years of heartbreak, hours
of agony, rivers of tears, into the life of this elder; and they would
have succeeded in dividing the church except for his faithfulness.
Men with less strength of character would have abandoned the flock
to this pack of wolves, but because one devout elder could not be
moved from righteousness, the congregation was saved from de-
stroying itself. The preacher moved on, but soon thereafter the elder
died. However, the fruits of his grievous labor lived on, towards
eternity.

Two illustrations are truthfully related of the help wrought to
elders by preacher's wisely and scripturally defending the respect
due to elders. The first is an incident where an eldership was in disagreement as to whether or not a young preacher could successfully accomplish their work. They effected a compromise in the agreement to hire the youthful man for a duration of three months. This
minister's work was so well done, as to please the entire membership, that he was employed for an indefinite stay with this church.
The ensuing chain of events was, no doubt, begun because of the elder's discussion relative to the preacher's trial period becoming known
by individual members. Ill feelings were displayed against one of the
elders who had not been in favor of hiring the young man, with
some members disrespectfully avoiding the elder. A devout man in
the church showed loving respect in his action of informing the
preacher, in quiet confidence, about the existing attitudes toward
this elder. The results of the preacher's disposition was good will,
with attentive love, extended to the elder. Harmony was restored within the church membership, by the close friendship between this good

elder and wise young minister, that could not have come into being if the preacher had not been a man after God's own heart and had joined the force of criticism. Another case was in a preacher's wise discernment of the disrespectful dislike for one of the elders, by the church members, when he began his work with them. The infantile action of some of the members was displayed in their audible noises—sighs, rattling papers, shuffling of feet—whenever this elder spoke in the assembly. Such action was intolerable and inexcusable, irrespective of previous provocation; two wrongs can never make anything right. The wisdom of decision and of action on the part of the newly arrived preachers' determination to gain, by according, respect for this elder was rewarded. For years thereafter the elder served this church, and died as he had lived, with honor, esteemed by all the members.

A RIGHTEOUS RELATIONSHIP

The personification of a righteous relationship between all Christians in the household of faith abides in a certain church, related here for illustration. The elders are outstanding men, of ordinary human abilities, dedicated to the Lord and the church they shepherd. The preacher is renowned for his fidelity to the work of the Lord's people and his abiding respect for the elders. Neither the elders nor the preacher will countenance, nor tolerate, disrespectful criticism about one another. They are harmoniously united, as devoted servants, to their co-labor, bound with the tie of Christian love. They will, at times, agree to disagree, but after the freedom of expressed opinions has been granted, there is no lingering resentment one for the other. The confidence of their joint-sanctuary, of eldership meetings, is protected by all. The deacons serving this church are honored for their work; appreciating their rightful position as being assistants to their elders. The inhabitants of this congregation have the full assurance that the programming of their work is well done, and deserving of their wholehearted support. Whatever the proposed program, these members endorse it without quibbling;

whether the work involves the spending of several hundred-thousand dollars, or months of arduous toil, they neither criticize nor complain. The relationship of this church is according to the Lord's plan: Member-backed leadership, and leader-backed membership! The work of this congregation is individual, collective, a delight, and produces abundant fruit because it is fixed in the center of Godliness.

Absolute submission to the leadership of a church, by the membership, as dedicated men who are submissive to the Lord's Divine Will, is to honor God and glorify His name on earth. A church composed of this loving attitude cannot be shaken by outside pressure, foes, or opposition. Fear is born of internal sources, not external pressure, and greater is the power within a united congregation than is contained in all the forces of the world. . ."For the Lord God will help me; therefore shall I not be confounded."